CLAN AND CASTLE

THE LIVES AND LANDS OF SCOTLAND'S GREAT FAMILIES

Chris Tabraham, Principal Historian

Scotland's castles are magnificent and astonishing. Whether rising impregnable from volcanic crags, dominating the shores of sea, loch or river, or standing in stoic isolation on barren moorland, they capture the eye and fire the imagination. What events have they witnessed over the centuries? What did they look like in their heyday? Above all, perhaps, who built them and why? This book provides some of the answers to those questions.

It does so in the context of Scotland's ancient family groupings, known as clans. Clan members shared not only a common ancestry, but also their social structures, their territories and their customs. Clan allegiance was a powerful social bond, particularly in the Highlands. The story of a Scottish castle is therefore inseparable from the story of the clan or clans who owned it.

This book focuses on seven great families – and Scotland's royal dynasties – to show how the castles that dominate our landscape were shaped by the clans who dominate our history.

Left: Detail from a Campbell of Glenorchy family tree by George Jamesone, dated 1635.

CONTENTS

Top: Queen Mary's Room at the Palace of Holyroodhouse, in a drawing by R. W. Billings.

Front cover: Castle Campbell in its impressive location overlooking Dollar Glen, Clackmannanshire.

INTRODUCTION

The castles of Scotland are as dramatic and inspiring as the landscape they inhabit. But they can only be fully understood in the context of the clans. From the earliest days, family bonds were at the heart of Scotland's social structures. The Gaelic word *clann* means 'children' or 'descendants', and membership is based on descent from a common ancestor.

Clans also produced offshoots, called cadets. On occasion, these outgrew the senior bloodline, as in the case of the MacDonalds. This gave rise to internal rivalries, between cousin and cousin if not brother and brother. Over centuries, clans prospered or weakened, and new loyalties were forged through expedient marriage, political alliance or financial necessity. Clans were held together by a complex network of relationships, but still at heart considered themselves bonded by kinship.

Insignia were adopted to identify individuals with their clans. Distinct tartans for each clan are a relatively recent invention, though tartan itself dates back many centuries. Similarly ancient are the plant badges – sprigs of a particular plant worn in clansmen's bonnets as a simple identifier of clan membership. Each clan also has its own crest and slogan.

Clans are associated mainly with the Highlands – the Gaelic-speaking northern and western parts of Scotland, including the Western Isles. But the families of southern Scotland wielded their influence in similar ways. It was not uncommon for Lowland families to be rewarded with Highland estates after backing the right side in a struggle for the throne. Both the Gordons and the Frasers originated in the Lowlands but became major clans of NE Scotland, thanks to their support for Robert I during the Wars of Independence in the 14th century.

Of course, many clans were indigenous. The Kennedys were native to Galloway and acted as a foil to incomers, including the Bruces. And the Campbells claim descent from the ancient Britons of Strathclyde. But some of the most prominent clans have Continental ancestry. The Douglases probably originated in Flanders, and the great Stewart dynasty – which ruled Scotland for over 300 years, and latterly England too – had its ancestral roots in Brittany, arriving here in the wake of William the Conqueror.

Castles belong to the age when military feudalism held sway. They were built by powerful lords who held land of the Crown in return for providing military service. Castles were visible statements of military might. But they were not the first impressive stone strongholds to appear in Scotland. The tall, stone broch towers built across northern Scotland a thousand years earlier can be seen as the ancestor of the medieval castle.

Left: The broch at Mousa in Shetland, at 13 metres the most impressive of Scotland's surviving Iron-Age strongholds.

Right: Alexander MacDonald, Lord of the Isles, depicted as a severe-faced tyrant by the Victorian artist R. R. Mclan.

But while we know brochs are unique to Scotland, we know nothing about who built them, and next to nothing about the nature of society then existing.

The medieval castle was well defended, but it also had an administrative role. It was a public arena, the centre of its lord's estate, from which he maintained law and order locally. His tenants came here to pay their rents and to fulfil their lord's military commitments. The castle was also the spiritual home of the clan. This was perhaps nowhere more true than at Finlaggan, which lay at the heart of the vast MacDonald hegemony throughout the later Middle Ages.

Down the centuries, castle-building developed in response to changes in the fabric of society, and advances in military technology. With the advent of gunpowdered artillery in the early 16th century, castles began to be equipped with yawning gunholes. But by then, the feudal system was fading fast, freeing landowners to adopt a more private way of life. Thus, tasteful embellishment emerged as a more pressing consideration than defence. Many castles were in active use for centuries and were adapted time and again, according to the requirements of each era.

This book is not intended as an exhaustive study of the castle, or indeed the clan. It tells the stories of seven of Scotland's more powerful families to explore castle-building across the country.

We encourage readers to discover Scotland's castles for themselves. The major castles of each clan are shown on a map within each chapter; while directions, Ordnance Survey map references and telephone numbers are given at the back of the book. We invite readers to marvel at these magnificent monuments, but also to ponder the lives of the lords who built them, and those of their kin who defended them. This book is here to help unravel their stories.

Andrew Burnet
Editor

CASTLES
ROYAL

This page: Edinburgh, one of Scotland's most formidable royal castles.

Opposite (top): Malcolm III, founder of the Canmore dynasty.

Opposite (margin): The earliest royal arms of Scotland.

Opposite (bottom): A penny showing the head of Alexander III, minted around 1290.

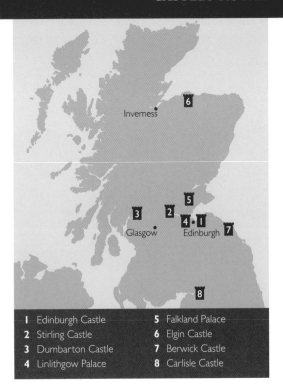

1	Edinburgh Castle	5	Falkland Palace
2	Stirling Castle	6	Elgin Castle
3	Dumbarton Castle	7	Berwick Castle
4	Linlithgow Palace	8	Carlisle Castle

CASTLES OF THE CANMORES

Castles appeared in Britain following the Norman Conquest of England in 1066. William the Conqueror built the first one, near the battlefield of Hastings. Castles were an instrument of feudalism, and could only be built by the king and those subjects holding land in return for military service.

In 1052 King MacBeth had enlisted Norman knights to help him retain his grip on power. They didn't stay long enough to settle and build castles, for most were killed at Dunsinane, near Perth, in 1054. MacBeth's opponent that day, Malcolm, became king himself in 1058. Known to his people as Canmore, 'Great Chief' (from the Gaelic *ceann mór*), Malcolm III remained implacably opposed to the Normans throughout his long reign and died fighting them in England in 1093. By then, their new-fangled castles had become prominent in the English landscape. It wasn't long before they were making their mark in Scotland also.

There was no Norman Conquest of Scotland. On the contrary, the Normans were invited to settle here by Malcolm's successors, notably his youngest son, David, who became king in 1124. Born in the royal residence at Dunfermline, young David had travelled to England with his sister, Maud, for her marriage to the future Henry I. When he returned some 20 years later he was thoroughly imbued with Norman culture and mightily impressed by their castles. He built quite a number throughout his realm.

They included Edinburgh, on the Castle Rock where his mother, Queen Margaret, had died after receiving the tragic news of her husband's death; Peebles, where his eldest son, Prince Henry, died unexpectedly in 1152; and Carlisle, where he himself died in the following year.

Carlisle was not the only Scottish royal castle built in what is now England. Berwick was Scotland's most important royal castle by far, until effectively lost to England during the Wars of Independence in the early 14th century. David's successors, Malcolm IV and William I, followed his lead, and by the time of William's death at Stirling Castle in 1214, there were royal castles the length and breadth of the kingdom. The two Alexanders, II and III, who reigned for most of the 13th century, spent vast sums transforming these modest residences into formidable stone strongholds.

Sadly, little remains of any of them today, other than the rocky knolls and grassy mounds on which they were built – with two notable exceptions: David's lofty stone keep still dominates Carlisle Castle, and little St Margaret's Chapel in Edinburgh Castle, which David built to his mother's memory, is now the oldest building in the city. We don't have far to look for the reason – the bitter and bloody Wars of Independence with England.

Left: The great stone keep (centre right) at Carlisle Castle in England was built by David I of Scotland.

Margin: The royal arms of John Balliol (shown with a broken crown to represent his discredited reign) and those of his rival and successor Robert I, 'the Bruce'.

Below: Robert the Bruce, represented as a national hero in a 20th-century statue at Edinburgh Castle.

CASTLES UNDER THE BALLIOLS AND BRUCES

The tragic death in 1290 of seven-year-old Margaret, the 'Maid of Norway', en route to Scone for her enthronement as Queen of Scots, brought the curtain down on the Canmore dynasty. No sooner had her body been returned to Norway for burial than the rival contenders began to throw their hats into the ring – all 13 of them. Most were rank outsiders, but two were joint-favourites – John Balliol, Lord of Galloway, and Robert Bruce, Lord of Annandale (not the King Robert but his grandfather, known as 'the Competitor').

Edward I of England, brother-in-law of the late Alexander III, was invited by the Scots to help determine the succession, and in 1292, at Berwick Castle, he pronounced his verdict – John Balliol. Two weeks later, on St Andrew's Day (30 November), King John was enthroned at Scone on the Stone of Destiny. Four years later came disaster. Edward, furious that the Scots had effectively sidelined his 'puppet-king', invaded Scotland at the head of a huge army, defeated the Scots at Dunbar, forced Balliol to abdicate near Montrose, and returned over the Border with the Scottish Crown Jewels and the Stone of Destiny.

So began the Wars of Independence that would rumble on for the next 60 years.

There wasn't much castle-building during all that time, and what little there was can be attributed to Edward and his Plantagenet heirs. Visitors to Lochmaben Castle, Dumfriesshire, will see the ruins of a castle begun by Edward I and completed by his grandson, Edward III; its English garrison was finally kicked out in 1384 when Archibald 'the Grim', 3rd Earl of Douglas, successfully stormed its formidable defences.

That left just two Scottish castles in English hands, Berwick and Roxburgh, in the eastern Borders. Little remains of either, but what does was probably built by the English – the impressive Constable's Tower at Berwick, bristling with fishtailed arrowslits, and the meagre masonry fragments on top of Roxburgh's great mound, built and paid for by Richard II.

The Scots, far from building castles, did their utmost to destroy them. When Robert Bruce, grandson of the Competitor, became Robert I in 1306, he knew that he couldn't possibly beat the English in pitched battle – not yet

Right: The royal seals of (clockwise from right) David I, William I 'the Lion' and Alexander II.

Far right: The ruins of Berwick Castle, Scotland's most important castle before the 14th-century wars with England. It now lies just south of the Anglo-Scottish border.

anyway – so he adopted scorched-earth tactics. And so, one by one, royal castles across Scotland, from Dumfries to Nairn and Ayr to Aberdeen, were recaptured and demolished. By the time of Bannockburn in 1314 only mighty Berwick and Stirling remained in English hands. An English chronicler, writing of the loss of Roxburgh in the spring of 1314, bemoaned: 'all that beautiful castle the Scots pulled down to the ground, like the other castles that they had succeeded in capturing, lest the English should ever again rule the land by holding the castle'.

In 1357, Bruce's son, David II, returned to Scotland after prolonged captivity in the Tower of London. His reappearance brought to an end the Wars of Independence, and the Scots began to rebuild their shattered lives – and their castles. David himself took the lead, embarking on a major rebuilding of Edinburgh Castle; with Berwick lost to England, Edinburgh now became Scotland's principal royal castle and burgh. David died at Edinburgh Castle in 1371 without seeing his new fortress completed. That pleasure fell to his successor, Robert II, first of the Royal Stewarts.

DID YOU KNOW...

Robert Bruce probably never lived in any of his royal castles, preferring to demolish them rather than see them in enemy hands. In his last three years, he lived in a modest manor house at Cardross, on the River Leven, Dunbartonshire. The records tell of a hall, a chapel and chambers for the king and queen, with plastered walls, glazed windows and thatched roofs. Around the house were gardens and a park where he indulged his passion for hunting and hawking. He died there in 1329, in his 55th year.

ROYAL DYNASTIES

1058	**Malcolm III** ascends throne and founds Canmore dynasty.
1113	Malcolm's youngest son, **David I**, starts building castles.
1220	**Alexander II** builds Dumbarton Castle against threat from Norway.
1241	**Alexander III** born at Roxburgh Castle.
1290	**Margaret 'Maid of Norway'** dies off Orkney, ending Canmore dynasty.
1292	**John Balliol** ascends throne and founds Balliol dynasty.
1296	**John deposed by Edward I** of England. Berwick and other royal castles fall into English hands.
1306	**Robert I (Bruce)** ascends throne, founds Bruce dynasty and acquires castles forfeited by enemies, including Urquhart and Dunstaffnage.
1314	**Bruce** retakes Roxburgh and Edinburgh Castles in build-up to Bannockburn. Stirling retaken after battle.
1371	**David II** dies at Edinburgh Castle. Robert the Steward ascends throne as **Robert II** and founds Stewart dynasty. Builds Dundonald Castle.
1424	**James I** builds new palace at Linlithgow following devastating fire.
1460	**James II** retakes Roxburgh but is killed by one of his own guns.
1482	**James III** finally loses Berwick to England.
1501	**James IV** builds new palaces at Holyrood and Falkland.
1503	**James IV** builds great hall in Stirling Castle to celebrate marriage to **Margaret Tudor.**
1511	**James IV** builds great hall in Edinburgh Castle to mark birth of **Prince Arthur**.

CASTLES OF THE ROYAL STEWARTS

The Royal Stewarts reigned for 343 years, by far the longest of any dynasty. James V, seventh in the line, predicted that his dynasty would 'end wi' a lass', which it did, though not with the lass he had in mind – his own daughter Mary. Only with the death of his great-great-great granddaughter, Anne, in 1714 did the dynasty finally die out. By then, Scotland and England had become one United Kingdom, and castles were largely a thing of the past.

When Robert, the 7th Steward of Scotland, ascended the throne as Robert II in 1371, the number of royal castles had been drastically reduced as a result of the wars with England. Most 12th-century strongholds had been so badly damaged that they were simply abandoned, and are now visible only as grassy mounds.

One example is Lanark Castle, whose English keeper, William de Haselrig, was ambushed and killed by William Wallace in 1297, helping spark the fightback against Edward I. Only a hard core remained, chief among them the mighty fortresses at Edinburgh, Stirling and Dumbarton. Other castles formerly in baronial hands had come under royal control as the result of forfeiture; they included such strongholds as Urquhart, on Loch Ness, once a seat of the powerful Comyn lords of Lochaber, and Dunstaffnage, in Argyll, built by the MacDougalls of Lorn. The Royal Stewarts were soon adding to their number.

Robert II was getting on in years by the time he ascended the throne, and understandably reluctant to leave his native west of Scotland for the political maelstrom of Edinburgh. So he built his own royal castle at Dundonald, on a prominent Ayrshire hill a little inland from the Firth of Clyde. 'King Bob' died there in 1390, as did his hapless son, Robert III, in 1406; a kick from a horse had so badly affected the latter that for most of his reign the Scots were governed by Robert, Duke of Albany,

Left: Dumbarton Castle on the Firth of Clyde, originally built by Alexander II to guard western Scotland from the Norwegians.

Right: A silver groat, minted around 1380, shows the head of Robert II.

the king's younger brother. Albany ruled from his own specially-built 'royal' castle of Doune, west of Stirling.

Dundonald and Doune couldn't be more different. Dundonald Castle is closed-up and inward-looking, reflecting its builder's withdrawn personality. By contrast, Doune Castle mirrors its extrovert master, of whom a contemporary, Abbot Walter of Inchcolm, wrote: 'Albany was kind, talkative and friendly, a daily attender of feasts, outstanding beside all his companions, a man who was a big spender and generous to strangers.' Doune remains a lasting testimony to the man known to history as 'Scotland's uncrowned king'.

ROYAL DYNASTIES CONT.

1512	**James V** born at Linlithgow Palace.
1532	**James V** builds new residence at Holyrood Palace.
1537	**James V** embellishes Falkland Palace to celebrate marriage to Madeleine de Valois.
1540	**James V** builds palace in Stirling Castle to celebrate marriage to Marie de Guise.
1542	**Mary Queen of Scots** is born at Linlithgow Palace, a week before James V dies at Falkland.
1566	**Mary** gives birth to **James VI & I** in Edinburgh Castle.
1573	'Lang Siege' of Edinburgh Castle ends after 18 months. **Regent Morton** builds Half-Moon Battery.
1594	**James VI** builds new chapel royal in Stirling Castle.
1600	**Charles I** born in Dunfermline Palace, last sovereign born in Scotland.
1617	**Palace** in Edinburgh Castle rebuilt for James VI's 'hamecoming'.
1633	**Charles I** last monarch to sleep in a Scottish royal castle, Edinburgh, the night before his Scottish coronation.
1650	**Oliver Cromwell** captures Edinburgh Castle.
1670s	**Charles II** rebuilds Holyrood Palace.
1708	**Stirling Castle's** defences strengthened following Jacobite Rising.
1714	**Queen Anne** dies, ending Stewart dynasty. Succeeded by **George I**, founder of Hanoverian dynasty.
1730s	Defences at **Dumbarton** and **Edinburgh** strengthened to counter Jacobite threat.
1746	**Stirling Castle** last castle besieged in Britain during '45 Jacobite Rising.

DID YOU KNOW...

When Alexander II built Dumbarton Castle in the 1220s, the nearest foreign country was not England, 90 miles (140km) to the south, but Norway, which then owned lands 14 miles (22km) to the west. Although the formidable stronghold would later become a bulwark against the English aggressor, it was built originally to help defend the country from the Norwegians.

Left: Linlithgow Palace, originally built by James I in the 15th century, and transformed by his descendants into one of Scotland's most luxurious royal residences.

Right: The royal crest on the gatehouse at Falkland Palace in Fife.

Below: James IV, arguably the most successful and cultured of the Stewart monarchs, whose building projects helped establish him as the 'Renaissance King'.

Four years after Regent Albany's death in 1420, the rightful king, James I, son of Robert III, returned to Scotland following lengthy captivity in England. No sooner had he settled in than a great fire swept through the royal burgh of Linlithgow, destroying the burgh kirk and badly damaging the royal castle. James turned tragedy into triumph. He turned his back on the medieval past, with its forbidding castles, and instead erected a majestic pleasure palace that would leave his subjects gazing open-mouthed in admiration. It was a statement in stone that this king, and this dynasty, was set on a far loftier plane than all others.

By the beginning of 1425 the builders were on site; by 1429 sufficient progress had been made to enable James to entertain the Archbishop of Reims there. By 1434 payments to Matthew, the king's painter, hint that finishing touches were being applied to the feast of sculpture gracing the outside walls, and the ceilings and walls within. By the time of James's assassination in 1437, one tenth of the king's income had been spent on Linlithgow Palace alone.

The creation of Linlithgow Palace set a benchmark that succeeding Royal Stewarts strove to emulate. But although the next two Jameses, II and III, spent considerable sums on improving and beautifying the ancient royal castles, both were outshone by James IV, Scotland's 'Renaissance King'.

James chose Stirling Castle as the principal stage on which he would impress the other crowned heads of Europe, not least his father-in-law, Henry VII of England, whose daughter, Margaret, he married in 1503. He built a monumentally impressive entrance gatehouse, now sadly much reduced in height, but originally resembling a classical triumphal arch. His guests would process through this arch as they made their way to his equally monumental great hall, by far the largest ever built in Scotland.

He didn't stop there. At Edinburgh, he grasped the opportunity presented by the decline of the monasteries to muscle in on the Augustinians of Holyrood Abbey and build there a new residence to replace his 'windy and right unpleasant' castle at the other end of the Royal Mile. At Falkland, across the Firth of Forth in Fife, he built a brand-new country seat where he could enjoy hawking and hunting. And he left his considerable mark elsewhere, most notably at Rothesay, his ancestral seat on Bute, where he built a new hall-gatehouse. How could one better that?

Left: Falkland Palace, embellished by James V to celebrate his first marriage, to Madeleine de Valois. He died there, aged 30, a week after the birth of his daughter, Mary Queen of Scots.

Above: James V with his second wife Marie de Guise. Like his father, James IV, he sponsored some of Scotland's most impressive palace architecture.

Well, the Renaissance King's son managed it. James V enhanced his father's creation at Stirling by adding a sumptuously ornate palace to celebrate his own marriage to Marie de Guise in 1538. He also lavishly embellished both of his father's new palaces at Holyrood and Falkland, adding a tennis court at the latter. Following his death at Falkland in 1542, all his daughter, Mary Queen of Scots, had to do was enjoy them, and she tried her best to do so during her short, tragic reign. One of the few rays of sunshine came in June 1566 when she gave birth to her only child, the future James VI; yet even this moment was beset by problems, for Mary had to forsake the enhanced comfort of her father's new residence at Holyrood for the increased security offered by Edinburgh Castle.

James VI's reign marked a watershed for Scotland's castles royal, for when he left for London in 1603 to be crowned James I of England also, Scotland became bereft of its sovereigns. It was as though someone had extinguished the lights in the castles and pleasure palaces of the Royal Stewarts. Just one overnight stop would be made by a reigning sovereign during the next 250 years – by

Charles I at Edinburgh Castle in 1633, the night before his Scottish coronation.

The redundant royal castles became little more than military garrisons, the once-impressive great halls in Stirling and Edinburgh converted into soldiers' barracks, and the palaces into quarters for their commanding officers. The defences too had to be rebuilt to counter the threats posed by Cromwell in the 1650s and the Jacobites in the early 18th century. Siege followed siege, until the guns finally fell silent in February 1746; Bonnie Prince Charlie's desultory siege of Stirling Castle proved to be the last inflicted on any castle in Scotland – indeed in all Britain.

DID YOU KNOW...

Scotland's first recorded fireworks display was held at Stirling Castle on the evening of 19 December 1566. It was the spectacular climax to a three-day celebration of the baptism of Mary Queen of Scots' only child, Prince James (the future James VI & I). It was preceded by a mock siege of an enchanted castle on the open ground in front of the mighty royal castle. The whole event was so expensive that Mary had to borrow heavily to pay for it.

CLAN
STEWART

This page: Blair Castle in Perthshire, one of the finest Stewart castles.

Opposite: A detail from the Bayeux Tapestry shows the Castle of Dol in Brittany, where the ancestors of the Stewarts served as stewards.

'Here Stuarts once in glory reigned,
And laws for Scotland's weal ordained.'
Robert Burns

Left: Oak, the plant badge of the Stewarts.

Below: The Stewart crest badge. The Latin motto translates as, 'Courage grows strong at the wound'.

THE STORY OF CLAN STEWART

In the late 11th century, a gentleman called Alan fitzFlaald arrived in England from Brittany. He joined Henry I's household and became a wealthy lord. When he died he left three sons. The eldest, Jordan, inherited the family's Brittany estates, while the second, William, became lord of the English patrimony. The youngest, Walter, seeing little prospect of advancement in either country, decided to chance his luck in David I's Scotland. It proved an astute move. While Jordan's line never rose above the knightly class, and William's descendants became earls of Arundel, Walter fitzAlan founded a dynasty that would one day rule not just in Scotland but over all Great Britain.

Everyone has a surname nowadays, but in 12th-century Scotland they weren't at all common. Most people were known by their Christian name and further identified by their father's name – as in Kenneth MacAlpin or Walter fitzAlan. Another way of distinguishing between people of the same name was to bestow nicknames that seemed apt, such as 'the Conqueror' and 'the Lion' – or, for the less lucky, 'Flatnose' and 'Twisted Mouth'. It was also becoming more common to link a person to the place they either hailed from (e.g. Robert 'de Bruce', from Brus, now Brix, in Normandy) or lived in (e.g. Archibald 'of Douglas', in Upper Clydesdale). The practice of taking the surname from one's occupation (for example, lorimer, meaning harness-maker) was only just catching on. One of the first families to do so were the Stewarts.

Soon after settling in Scotland, Walter fitzAlan (died 1177) was appointed King David's steward, responsible for running the royal household. The appointment was not unexpected; Walter's forebears had served as stewards of the counts of Dol, back in Brittany. Walter clearly did a good job, for the post soon became hereditary. Walter, the 3rd Steward, was the first to adopt the surname Stewart. By then they had already made a considerable mark on Scottish political life.

As well as making Walter his steward, King David lavished on him large estates across southern Scotland, centred on Renfrewshire and north Ayrshire. Walter had brought many of his own knights with him from England, and these too made Scotland their home. They included two from his Shropshire estates – Ralph de L'isle, ancestor of the Lyles, and Richard le Walleis 'the Welshman', whose most famous descendant was William Wallace – the celebrated patriot.

David's largesse was more than mere reward for loyal service. In the 12th century, the Firth of Clyde was the border between Scotland and Norway. David's elder brother, King Edgar, had ceded sovereignty over the Hebrides to King Magnus 'Barelegs' in 1098. David needed someone dependable to help defend his realm from the descendants of the Vikings, and to begin reclaiming the lost territories. Walter the Steward and his heirs didn't disappoint.

In 1164, Walter repulsed a huge armada of ships flying the flag of the mighty Somerled as it sailed past his castle at Renfrew. The self-styled 'King of the Isles' – ancestor of the MacDonalds – was killed early in the battle and the Steward had his head taken to Glasgow Cathedral as a trophy.

Somerled's demise proved the turning-point. By 1200 Alan, the 2nd Steward, had retaken the island of Bute for Scotland. The Norwegian kings were forced to act. An abortive invasion in 1230 was followed by a second in 1263, with Hakon IV commanding the fleet in person. Late that September he sailed into the Clyde and fought a bloody but indecisive skirmish with Alexander, the 4th Steward, at Largs. Hakon was forced to withdraw, beaten back more by the Scottish weather than by the Scottish Steward. As the Steward watched Hakon's fleet sail away, he could not know that this was the last the Scots would see of the Norwegians in the west of Scotland.

No sooner had the Stewarts helped their sovereign see off one predator than they were called on to help repel another. The Wars of Independence with England that erupted in 1296 almost obliterated Scotland as an independent nation. Its survival was down to many heroes, sung and unsung. Foremost among them were the Stewarts. James, the 5th Steward, fought alongside his liegeman Wallace at Falkirk (1298), and became one of Robert Bruce's greatest stalwarts. In gratitude, Bruce bestowed special favour on his teenage son, Walter, the 6th Steward, giving him command, jointly with Sir James Douglas, of a brigade at Bannockburn (1314). In its victorious aftermath, Bruce gave Walter his daughter Marjorie's hand in marriage.

That single act proved the making of the Stewarts, for baby Robert, born in March 1316, in due course became king himself.

Even before the Stewarts became 'royal', the family had spread its wings and flown far from the Renfrewshire nest. Among the first was Walter, the 4th Steward's younger brother. In 1261, he acquired through marriage the earldom of Menteith, west of Stirling. Walter's patrimony included not just the Trossachs heartlands but lands way to the west, including Knapdale, in Argyll.

Another notable descendant was John, the 4th Steward's second son, who became lord of Bonkyl, in Berwickshire, and fell at the Battle of Falkirk in 1298. The seven sons he sired produced an immense legacy. From them sprang the Stewart earls of Angus, Galloway (the present clan chief) and Lennox (whose most famous son was Darnley, Mary Queen of Scots' second husband) and the branches of Appin, Lorn and Innermeath, and Rosyth.

When the 7th Steward became Robert II in 1371, the family's prosperity grew, thanks to the vast assets available to the sovereign. They were showered with lands and titles, most of them forfeited by other noble dynasties, such as the Black Douglases. The Stewarts were the recipients of the first four Scottish dukedoms ever created, as well as 16 earldoms. These were augmented in the 16th century by wealthy benefices from the ailing monasteries.

Left: The Stewart coat of arms.

THE STEWARTS

c.1100	**Alan fitzFlaald**, the Count of Dol's steward, enters Henry I of England's service.
c.1135	Alan's son, **Walter**, enters **David I's** service as steward of Scotland, and given extensive landholding centred on Renfrew Castle.
1164	**Walter** defeats the great Somerled, 'King of the Isles', near Renfrew.
c.1200	**Alan, 2nd Steward**, acquires the island of Bute and builds Rothesay Castle.
c.1210	**Walter, 3rd Steward**, adopts family surname of Stewart.
1230	**The Norwegians** capture Rothesay Castle after a bloody siege.
1261	**Walter**, brother of **Alexander, 4th Steward**, becomes Earl of Menteith.
1263	**Alexander** and **Walter** see off the Norwegian threat at Largs.
1298	**James, 5th Steward**, fights alongside **William Wallace** at Falkirk.
1314	**Walter, 6th Steward**, and **James of Douglas** lead brigade at Bannockburn.
1315	**Walter** marries Robert Bruce's daughter, **Princess Marjorie**.
1316	**Marjorie** gives birth to Robert (future **Robert II**).
1371	**Robert, 7th High Steward**, ascends throne as **Robert II.**
1390	**Alexander, Earl of Buchan**, 'The Wolf of Badenoch', burns Elgin Cathedral.
1398	**Robert II** makes his sons David and Robert dukes of Rothesay and Albany respectively.
c.1400	**Albany**, 'Scotland's uncrowned king', builds Doune Castle.
1425	Albany's son, **Murdoch**, executed for treason.
1570	**James, Earl of Moray** and Regent assassinated in Linlithgow.
1615	**Patrick, 2nd Earl of Orkney**, executed for treason in Edinburgh.
1714	**Queen Anne**, last of the Royal Stewarts, dies at Westminster, London.
1746	**The Stewarts** of Appin and Atholl fight for the Jacobites at Culloden.

Right: James Stewart, Earl of Moray, who governed Scotland as regent during the infancy of Mary Queen of Scots, but was assassinated in 1570.

Left: Dundonald Castle, Ayrshire, built by Robert II in 1371, on the site of an earlier castle built by his ancestor Alexander, 4th Steward.

James V alone gave commendatorships (lay abbacies) to all six of his illegitimate sons – some of whom were barely walking at the time. There was scarcely a corner of the realm where the Stewarts didn't cast a shadow. From Galloway to Shetland their names, titles, deeds and misdeeds dominate the pages of Scottish history.

For the scions of the House of Stewart were both famous and infamous. Among the former were two who served as governors of the realm, Robert, 1st Duke of Albany (died 1420), known to history as 'Scotland's uncrowned king', and John, 4th Duke of Albany (died 1536), who was raised in France and couldn't even speak the language. A third, James, Earl of Moray, served as regent from 1567 until his assassination three years later. Had he been James V's legitimate son, he would have succeeded Queen Mary, in place of her son, James VI.

Less admirable was the career of Alexander, 1st Earl of Buchan (died c. 1405), one of Robert II's 14 children and founder of the Stewarts of Atholl. He earned his soubriquet 'the Wolf of Badenoch' by leading his warband of 'wyld wykked Helandmen' out from their Cairngorm lair to burn and pillage across the Moray plain. Another notorious Stewart, Patrick, Earl of Orkney (executed 1615), earned his nickname 'Black Patie' by presiding over a reign of terror in his adopted Orkney and Shetland. So ungodly was he that his beheading in Edinburgh had to be delayed whilst he learned to recite the Lord's Prayer!

Given the privileges bestowed on their family, it might be expected that Stewarts would remain true to the cause of their royal kinsmen. But that was not always the case, notably during the Jacobite era, when James VII & II was exiled and his heirs, the 'Old' and 'Young' Pretender, attempted to re-establish the Stewart succession. When Culloden brought the Jacobite movement to a grim conclusion in 1746, there were many thousands of Stewarts in Scotland. But only the Stewarts of Atholl and Appin fought for the Jacobites.

Right: The effigy of Alexander Stewart, Earl of Buchan, who terrorised 14th-century Moray and became known as the Wolf of Badenoch.

CASTLES OF THE STEWARTS

Time has not been kind to the castles of the early Stewarts. Tarmacked roads now cover the remains of their chief seat at Renfrew, built by the 1st Steward on arriving in Scotland in the 1130s. It was near here that he overcame the mighty Somerled in 1164. We can only guess that it took the form of a great earthwork surrounded by water-filled moats and surmounted by a timber palisade and buildings.

Fortunately the castle of Robert Croc, one of Walter's knightly tenants in his Honour of Renfrew, has survived the rigours of time, to give us some idea as to what Renfrew Castle might have looked like. Crookston ('Croc's place'), near Paisley, still dominates its surroundings from its position on the crown of a hill and still retains its impressive encircling ditch. The ground within is now graced by the tall stone tower house built around 1400 by Sir John Stewart of Darnley, kinsman of Robert III.

Not much more remains of the 1st Steward's second stronghold, Dundonald, near Kilmarnock in Ayrshire. However, the 2nd Steward built a castle on Bute around 1200 which stands remarkably intact. And what a castle. Not only was Rothesay one of Scotland's earliest masonry castles, it was also unique in being circular. Only a handful of circular castles were built in Britain, the most famous being Windsor, built by Henry I, Alan fitzFlaald's erstwhile employer. Another, at Arundel in West Sussex, passed into the hands of the 3rd Steward's kinsman, John FitzAlan, Earl of Oswestry, in 1243.

Rothesay's shape is not its only unique feature. Immured in a later heightening of the curtain wall is the original crenellated, or notched, parapet from which the garrison twice defended the castle against the might of Norway. In 1230 the Norwegians dodged the arrows and boiling pitch and managed to hew their way through the wall with axes to gain entry. In 1263, prior to the debacle at Largs, the garrison surrendered without a fight. The castle's vulnerability to a fully pressed assault probably led the 4th Steward to add the four projecting round towers to the original curtain wall. The impressive rectangular gatehouse was added much later by his royal descendant, James IV, around 1500.

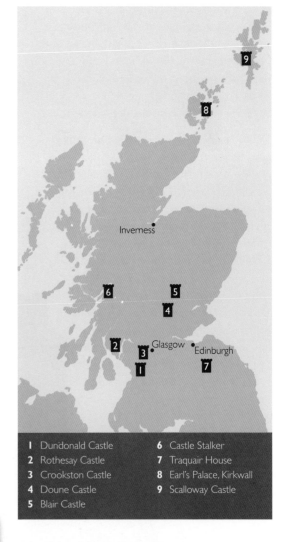

1	Dundonald Castle	6	Castle Stalker
2	Rothesay Castle	7	Traquair House
3	Crookston Castle	8	Earl's Palace, Kirkwall
4	Doune Castle	9	Scalloway Castle
5	Blair Castle		

Right: Crookston Castle, near Paisley, founded by Robert Croc, a tenant of Walter Stewart.

Left: Scalloway Castle, near Lerwick in Shetland.

Below: Doune Castle, built in its present forms by Robert Stewart, 1st Duke of Albany.

Below (inset): One of the gargoyles at Doune Castle.

In stark contrast is a castle associated with Albany's younger brother, Alexander, 'Wolf of Badenoch'. The island castle of Loch an Eilean, in the shadow of the Cairngorms, was the perfect bolthole for a royal son who went off the rails and extorted blackmail from the good bishop of Moray for questioning his marital fidelity. In 1390, after being excommunicated, the Wolf led his warband out from this island lair into the Moray plain, where they sent Elgin Cathedral up in flames; Bishop Bur bemoaned the destruction of that 'ornament of the realm, the glory of the kingdom'. It was the prelude to further disorder in the eastern Highlands, and descriptions of these marauders doing battle 'with their whole body clad in linen well daubed with wax or pitch and with an overcoat of deerskin' led to the word 'clan' becoming a derogatory term in Lowlanders' mouths. The mutual distrust between Highlander and Lowlander would ultimately help provoke the bloody slaughter on the battlefield of Culloden.

Around the time Alexander was adding those round towers to Rothesay, his younger brother, Walter Stewart, Earl of Menteith (died 1295), was building an equally impressive castle at Skipness, on his newly-acquired Knapdale estate, in Argyll. Here again the Stewarts created something unusual, for the array of crosslet-arrowslits through the west wall is the only systematic display of this type in Scotland. This form of arrowslit seems to have been a favourite of Walter's, for examples have recently been discovered at two more of his castles – Brodick, on Arran, and Doune, in the heart of his earldom of Menteith.

Doune is more usually associated with a later Stewart, Robert, 1st Duke of Albany, and governor on behalf of his feeble elder brother, Robert III. Albany held the reins of government for almost 20 years until his death in 1420 at the remarkable age of 80. A contemporary, Abbot Walter of Inchcolm, called him 'a big spender' and a man noted for his 'large tabling and belly cheer', and his castle at Doune is testimony to that. To stand in his cathedral-like great hall, and enter its vast kitchens and basement vaults, is to get as close as it is possible to get to one of Scotland's greatest medieval statesmen.

The Wolf's 'Helandmen' were probably drawn from a number of clans, but the Wolf himself founded his own, the Stewarts of Atholl, in Perthshire. Their chief seat became Blair Castle, near Dunkeld Cathedral where the Wolf was laid to rest around 1406. Blair has served as the chief residence of the earls and dukes of Atholl for centuries, but there is little behind its whitewashed veneer that is truly medieval, thanks to Cromwell's guns in the 1650s and its subsequent rebuilding.

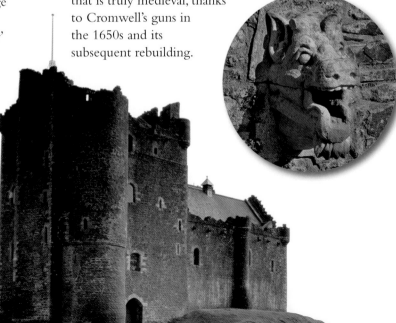

Right: One of the crosslet-arrowslits unique to Skipness Castle.

Far right: The elaborate Earl's Palace in Kirkwall, Orkney, built in the 16th century by the detested Earl Patrick Stewart, known as 'Black Patie'.

Another seat of the Stewart earls of Atholl, Balvenie Castle, in Glen Fiddich, has fared far better. John, the 4th Earl (died 1579) built a fine new lodging at one corner of the ancient castle built by the mighty Comyn lords in the 13th century. A stone panel gracing the entrance is emblazoned with his arms and family motto: *'Furth fortun and fil thi fatris'* – '[Go] forth fortune and fill thy coffers'. The earl welcomed Mary Queen of Scots to his new residence in 1562.

So far as we know, the chief of the Stewarts of Appin never welcomed such an important visitor to his stronghold Castle Stalker, sitting snugly on its tiny island of Eilean an Stalcaire 'island of the hunter' and guarding the sea-lane from Loch Linnhe into little Loch Laich – but it is possible that James V sailed past it during his naval expedition against the erstwhile Lords of the Isles in 1540.

Royal visitors do not appear to have graced any of the castles built by Patrick Stewart, Earl of Orkney and Lord of Shetland.

DID YOU KNOW...

Recent archaeological excavations at Dundonald, site of Robert II's impressive late-14th-century tower house, have uncovered remains of a formidable stone castle built by Alexander, the 4th Steward, in the later 13th century. His castle may even have surpassed mighty Bothwell Castle, for it had not one impressive twin-towered gatehouse but two, so mirroring Edward I of England's great castle at Rhuddlan, in North Wales. One gatehouse faced east into Scotland, and the other west, towards the distant islands of Arran and Bute, newly acquired by them from Norway. It was as if the Steward was displaying in stone and lime his family's success in extending the boundaries of Scotland.

Had they done so, they would have been amazed at their quality and sophistication, particularly the Earl's Palace in Kirkwall, justly hailed by W. Douglas Simpson as 'possibly the most mature and accomplished piece of Renaissance architecture left in Scotland'. James VI's decision not to visit was probably less to do with the distance than with the personality of his kinsman. 'Black Patie' was a nasty piece of work who exercised unimaginable tyranny over his island subjects. This included using them as slaves to build his Orcadian castles at Kirkwall and Birsay, and his Shetland bases at Scalloway and Jarlshof.

Royalty were much more inclined to visit the Lowland castles of their Stewart kinsmen. In 1586, Francis Stewart, 5th Earl of Bothwell, welcomed James VI to his new and innovative lodging at Crichton Castle, Midlothian. Just four years later, Francis tried to kidnap James as he slept in the Palace of Holyroodhouse. The Stewarts of Traquair, that wonderful castle near Peebles, frequently welcomed their royal cousins as overnight guests; they included Mary Queen of Scots and her second husband, Darnley, in 1566, not long before he met his explosive end at Kirk o'Field, in Edinburgh, and Prince Charles Edward in 1745, prior to his march into England. The story goes that he entered through the famous 'Bear Gates', and that when he left the Earl locked them, swearing that they would not be opened until a Stewart sat once more upon the throne of Great Britain. The 'steekit yetts' remain closed to this day.

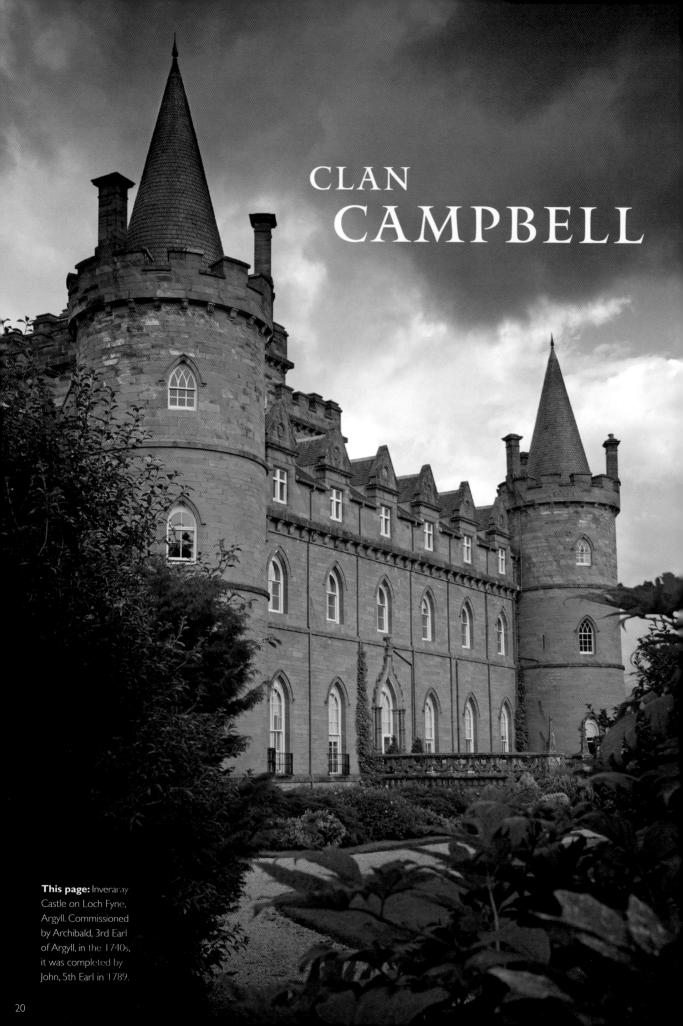

CLAN
CAMPBELL

This page: Inveraray Castle on Loch Fyne, Argyll. Commissioned by Archibald, 3rd Earl of Argyll, in the 1740s, it was completed by John, 5th Earl in 1789.

THE STORY OF CLAN CAMPBELL

The Campbells are one of Scotland's most famous – not to say infamous – clans. This is thanks in no small measure to their legendary, if overhyped, long-running bloodfeud with their fiercest rivals, the MacDonalds. If not perhaps the most popular Highland clan, the Campbells were certainly among the most successful, rising from comparative obscurity in the 13th century to become the most powerful clan in the western Highlands during the later Middle Ages. On the way, they disposed of the MacDougalls and the MacDonalds.

Later Campbell genealogies tell of the clan emerging from an earlier kindred called MacDuibne or O'Duibne ('sons of Duibne'), and even claim roots reaching back through the ancient Britons of Strathclyde to the legendary King Arthur. Their surname, originally spelt Cambel, derived from the Gaelic Caimbeul, 'crooked or twisted mouth', perhaps a characteristic of an ancient chief.

The clan's ancestral heartland is Argyll, and they may long have had a presence in the region. However, their recorded association with the county dates only from the later 13th century, and the first Campbell on record, Gillespic Campbell in 1263, had an estate in the heart of Scotland, at Menstrie, east of Stirling. By 1293, however, Gillespic's son, Cailean Mór – 'Big Colin' – was holding sway over the people of Loch Awe from the island stronghold of Innis Chonnell. This was the clan chief from whom all subsequent chiefs took their patronym MacCailean Mór – 'son

of Big Colin'. Alas, Colin was struck down by John MacDougall, Lord of Lorn, during a skirmish in the hills above Loch Awe; a humble stone cairn is said to mark the very spot.

The clan's meteoric rise to power effectively began with Cailean Mór's sons, who threw in their lot with King Robert Bruce during the bloody Wars of Independence in the early 14th century. One son, Neil, was instrumental in helping Bruce escape, following his defeat at Methven in 1306, to his famous encounter with a spider in an unidentified cave. Neil was handsomely rewarded, marrying Bruce's sister, Mary.

Thereafter, Neil's descendants built up their power-base in the west, courtesy of their close ties with the Bruces and Stewarts. Pivotal to their success was Neil's grandson, Gillespic 'of Arran'. His personal relationship with Robert the Steward resulted in the Campbells of Loch Awe acquiring a vast estate of lordships, stretching from the Firth of Clyde to the Firth of Lorn. On ascending the throne as Robert II, the erstwhile Steward and founder of the Stewart dynasty appointed his faithful henchman Campbell as hereditary royal lieutenant in Argyll.

Thereafter, the Campbells of Loch Awe acted as the Crown's eyes and ears in the problematic

Left: Innis Chonnell, on an island in Loch Awe, Argyll. This was the 13th-century stronghold of Cailean Mór.

Below: Three Campbell patriarchs, as depicted in the 17th-century *Black Book of Taymouth*. Duncan of Loch Awe (centre) is flanked by his son Colin of Glenorchy (right) and grandson Colin, 1st Earl of Argyll.

west, and were instrumental in the long and turbulent dismemberment of the empire of their great rivals, the MacDonald Lords of the Isles, who were finally forfeited in 1493.

By then, the Campbell chiefs were not only powerful regional lords; they had also taken up important positions at the heart of national government. This process culminated in 1483 with the appointment of Colin Campbell, 1st Earl of Argyll, as James III's chancellor. Throughout the 16th century, the Campbell chiefs continued to strut on the national stage. Following the Protestant Reformation in 1560, they wholeheartedly embraced the new religion and spearheaded the fight against those clans stubbornly refusing to conform.

Yet more territories in the west fell into their hands, including Kintyre, where in 1607 the 7th Earl established a Protestant 'plantation' at Campbeltown for James VI & I.

King James wasn't to know that the Campbells would soon play a leading role in the downfall of the Catholic clans – and of his blessed Stewart dynasty. Perhaps if he had listened to his own Bishop of the Isles, the course of history might have been diverted. The cleric wrote of the Campbells: 'Neither can I think it either good or profitable to his majesty … to make that name greater in the Isles than they are already or get to root out one pestiferous clan and plant in one little better.' Time and again in the 17th century, the Campbells fought against James's heirs for threatening to undo the Reformation settlement, and both the 1st Marquis (1661) and his son, the 9th Earl (1685), lost their heads on the scaffold for their beliefs.

Campbell misfortunes were reversed by the flight of Catholic James VII & II into exile in 1689, and his replacement on the throne by Protestant William of Orange. Thereafter they went from strength to strength, taking a lead role in the struggle between the government and the Jacobites, the supporters of James. They soon got down to business.

In late January 1692, soldiers from Argyll's Regiment marched out from Fort William and billeted in Glencoe, home of the MacIans of Glencoe, a sept of MacDonald Clanranald.

Above: The Campbell coat of arms.

They availed themselves of MacIan hospitality for 12 days until, at the given signal in the dead of night, they rose from their beds and slaughtered everyone they could find. Poor Alasdair MacIan was the first to be dispatched, gunned down in his nightshirt. His good lady, falling on his prone corpse, was stripped bare, dragged outside and left to die in the freezing snow. By dawn, 38 men, women and children lay dead. Glencoe, 'the narrow glen', had become 'the Glen of Weeping… melancholy, brooding, the very valley of the Shadow of Death,' as Thomas Macaulay put it in his epic *History of England*.

The Campbells were rewarded for their unfaltering loyalty. King William conferred a dukedom on the 10th Earl in 1701, and in due course the 2nd Duke became one of the first field marshalls appointed in the British Army. He led George I's troops into battle at Sheriffmuir against James Stuart, 'the Old Pretender', in the 1715 Jacobite Rising. Campbell's men were also there at the death of the Jacobite movement. In 1746, they became the only Highland clan to fight on the government side at Culloden, the battle that ended in defeat for the Pretender's son, Bonnie Prince Charlie. The end of the Jacobite dream resulted in the Campbell chiefs becoming undisputed leaders of the western Highlands.

Below: An artist's impression of Castle Campbell as it may have looked around 1550.

Above: Captain Robert Campbell of Glenlyon, who led the massacre of MacDonalds at Glencoe in 1692.

CASTLES OF THE CAMPBELLS

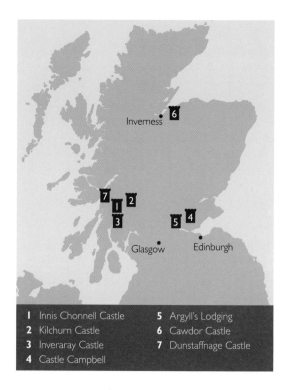

1 Innis Chonnell Castle
2 Kilchurn Castle
3 Inveraray Castle
4 Castle Campbell
5 Argyll's Lodging
6 Cawdor Castle
7 Dunstaffnage Castle

On a tiny island in Loch Awe stands gaunt, ivy-tangled Innis Chonnell Castle. This was the stronghold where Cailean Mór held sway before his untimely death at the hand of MacDougall of Lorn around 1296.

The stone castle, one of the oldest in Scotland, is powerfully impressive, even in its ruined state. Because of this, it somehow seems too mighty a castle to have been built by a relatively minor lord, such as any of the Campbells of the 12th and early 13th centuries. It may be that Cailean Mór was the first Campbell to reside there, in his capacity as keeper on behalf of Alexander III, and that the early 13th-century stronghold was actually built as a royal castle, or by the powerful MacDougall lords of Lorn.

Cailean Mór's forebears, however, would undoubtedly have had a castle, or castles, somewhere in the district, though less formidable than Innis Chonnell. One likely candidate is the intriguingly-named Caisteal na Nighinn Ruaidhe, 'castle of the red-haired maiden', on an islet in Loch Avich, west of Loch Awe. The maiden is thought to be Brigid, daughter of Dugal MacCaurre, *tòiseach* (chief) of Loch Avich. According to tradition, she married Dougal Campbell of Craignish, thus bringing the Loch Avich lands into the Campbell empire.

Incidentally, high in the hills above Loch Avich is Càrn Chailein, 'Colin's Cairn', marking the spot where Cailean Mór is said to have been murdered by MacDougall of Lorn, shot in the back by an arrow.

In 1445 Cailean Mór's descendant, Duncan Campbell, was created Lord Campbell by James II. Shortly thereafter, he took the bold decision to move the clan seat from landlocked Loch Awe to the salt waters of Loch Fyne. And there, at the mouth of the River Aray, he built a new castle, centred on a lofty tower house, as was the fashion of the day. Quite why he chose to forsake the ancient

heartland of Clan Campbell is unclear, but he may have needed to live more centrally within the now vast Campbell empire.

Duncan's growing involvement in national government also required him to make frequent journeys into the Lowlands, particularly the royal castles in Edinburgh and Stirling. Inveraray was far better placed for both purposes. Ancient Innis Chonnell wasn't abandoned altogether. It took on a new role as a grim prison for those falling foul of the Campbells. Its most famous inmate was Donald Dubh 'Black Donald', grandson of John, the last Lord of the Isles, who was incarcerated therein from his childhood until 'his hair got grey'.

Lord Campbell's grandson and successor, Colin, 1st Earl of Argyll, made a second, equally significant move around 1464. At this time, he married Elizabeth Stewart, thus acquiring Castle Gloom, impressively sited in the Ochil Hills east of Stirling.

Left: Dunstaffnage Castle on the Firth of Lorn, Argyll. Built in the 13th century by the MacDougalls, it came into Campbell ownership in 1470.

Renamed Castle Campbell in 1489, Gloom became the earl's principal Lowland seat, from where he was able to dance attendance on his king and carry out his duties as chancellor of Scotland. He and his successors added to, and embellished, the original tower house of the Stewarts of Lorn, to create one of Scotland's most impressive late-medieval castles. Mary Queen of Scots graced its portal with her presence in January 1563, as a guest attending the wedding of her kinsman, James Stewart, Lord Doune, to Margaret, the 5th Earl's sister.

Meanwhile, back in their native Argyll, the Campbell earls continued to expand their landed interests. Important, and lucrative, keeperships of royal castles fell into their laps, including Dunstaffnage (1470), Castle Sween (1481) and Skipness (1502). They left their mark on all of them. At Skipness they built the tall tower house that still dominates the formidable 13th-century stone curtain wall. At Dunstaffnage they completely redesigned the entrance gatehouse and built the 'new house' in the castle courtyard, where Flora MacDonald was briefly held prisoner after helping Prince Charles Edward Stuart escape following his defeat at Culloden. Numerous other castles were built with the consent of the Campbell chiefs, including Carnasserie, built around 1570 by John Carswell, Bishop of the Isles.

THE CAMPBELLS

1263	**Gillespic** the first Campbell to appear on record.
1293	Various Campbells holding lands in Argyll, including **Cailean Mór** ('Big Colin').
1309	Cailean's sons, **Neil** and **Donald**, attend Bruce's first parliament at St Andrews.
c.1314	**Neil** marries Bruce's sister, **Mary**.
1315	**Bruce** confirms Neil's son, **Colin**, in possession of Loch Awe and Ardscotnish.
1382	Neil's grandson, **Gillespic 'of Arran'**, appointed royal lieutenant in Argyll by Robert II.
1445	**Duncan** created Lord Campbell by James II. Transfers clan seat from Innis Chonnell to Inveraray.
1457	Duncan's grandson, **Colin**, created **Earl of Argyll** by James II.
c.1465	**1st Earl** acquires Castle Gloom (Castle Campbell) through marriage.
1470	**1st Earl** acquires Lordship of Lorn, and installs a kinsman as keeper of Dunstaffnage Castle.
1481	**1st Earl** appointed keeper of Castle Sween.
1483	**1st Earl** appointed chancellor by James III.
1499	**Archibald, 2nd Earl**, appointed keeper of Tarbert Castle.
1502	**2nd Earl** appointed keeper of Skipness Castle.
1513	**2nd Earl** killed at Flodden, with many other Campbells.
1576	**Colin, 6th Earl**, appointed chancellor by James VI.
1607	**Archibald, 7th Earl**, founds Campbeltown.

Right: Duncan Campbell, 7th Lord Glenorchy, known as 'Black Duncan of the Castles'.

Far right: Cawdor Castle, near Nairn, acquired by a son of the 3rd Earl in 1510. A 19th-century engraving by R. W. Billings.

CASTLES OF THE CADETS

Of the numerous Campbell cadets, undoubtedly the most important, and most powerful, were the Campbells of Glenorchy (later Earls of Breadalbane). Indeed, there were times when this branch almost rivalled the Campbells of Argyll for supremacy.

They originated in 1432 when Duncan (later 1st Lord Campbell) granted his second son, Colin, the lordship of Glenorchy, at the northern end of Loch Awe. This was a sweetener, to ensure his loyalty following the sudden death of his eldest son, Gillespic. And there, on 'Elankylequhurne', a low promontory projecting into the deep waters of the loch, Colin built his new residence. Kilchurn Castle is one of the most dramatically sited castles in Scotland. Viewed from the loch, with Ben Cruachan rising up behind, it mirrors perfectly the power and ambition of its new lord.

Colin of Glenorchy had no sooner moved into his impressive new towered castle than he was acquiring new estates. Shortly after attending James II's coronation at Holyrood Abbey in 1437, he was instrumental in capturing one of James I's assassins. The assassin's estate at Lawers on Loch Tay was forfeited, and the grateful king gave it to Sir Colin, thus luring him from his west Highland lair. Colin acquired further lands around Loch Tay, including Balloch (now Taymouth). A descendant, Duncan, 7th Lord Glenorchy (1545–1631), was an even more prodigious castle-builder, constructing impressive towers at Achallader, Barcaldine, Edinample, Finlarig and Loch Dochart. Little wonder he was known as 'Black Duncan of the Castles'.

One other cadet castle stands out for special mention – Cawdor. The lands of Cawdor, near Nairn, came into the Campbell empire in 1510 when the 2nd Earl's third son married the 12-year-old Muriel, heiress of the Thane of Cawdor. John Campbell acquired a fine new castle as well as a fine young wife, for

DID YOU KNOW...

Entombed within impressive Cawdor Castle lies a tree. According to legend, an ancient Thane of Cawdor dreamt that he was advised to build a new castle. Its location was to be determined by a donkey, heavily laden with a coffer of gold and left to roam the estate. Wherever it lay down to rest at the end of the day – that would be the place. It chose a spot under a hawthorn tree. Scientific analysis has recently shown that the ancient hawthorn is in fact a holly that died around 1372.

Right: Kilchurn Castle, on Loch Awe, Argyll, built in the 15th century by Colin Campbell of Glenorchy.

her immediate forebears had built a substantial tower house. The Campbells of Cawdor greatly added to it down the centuries, most notably Sir Hugh Campbell, 15th Thane, in the mid-17th century. His heraldic achievement is splendidly emblazoned in stone on the great chimneypiece in the Blue Room.

All these Campbell castles, whether built by the clan chiefs or their kinsmen, were constructed in an age when the need for defence was paramount. By the 17th century, such considerations were largely obsolete; even the 16th-century towers would have been seen as uncomfortable and unseemly residences for leading members of the aristocracy. And so they were abandoned by their masters.

Around 1670, Archibald, 9th Earl, relocated his Lowland seat from draughty Castle Campbell to an infinitely more amenable town house, Argyll's Lodging, on the approach to Stirling Castle. A century later, Archibald, 3rd Duke, moved from the old tower house at Inveraray into a splendid new mansion adjacent. Not to be outdone, John, 4th Earl of Breadalbane, had antique Balloch pulled down in the early 19th century and replaced it with the monumental Taymouth Castle, described in John Gifford's recent survey as 'a huge castellated status symbol'.

Inveraray and Taymouth may be superficially martial in appearance, but they were nothing other than great castellated country houses. With Taymouth the castle-building days of Clan Campbell were at an end.

THE CAMPBELLS CONT.

1641	**Archibald, 8th Earl**, created Marquis of Argyll by Charles I.
1651	**Marquis** places crown on **Charles II**'s head at Scone.
1652	**Marquis** acknowledges **Cromwell**'s United Commonwealth of England and Scotland.
1661	**Marquis** executed on orders of Charles II.
1681	**John of Glenorchy** created Earl of Breadalbane by Charles II.
1685	**Archibald, 9th Earl**, captured while leading a rising against James VII and executed.
1692	**Campbells** slaughter **MacDonalds** in the Massacre of Glencoe.
1701	**Archibald, 10th Earl**, created Duke of Argyll.
1715	**John, 2nd Duke**, commands government army at Sheriffmuir.
1746	**Campbells** only Highland clan to fight on government side at Culloden.
1748–61	**Archibald, 3rd Duke**, builds Inveraray Castle.

CLAN
DOUGLAS

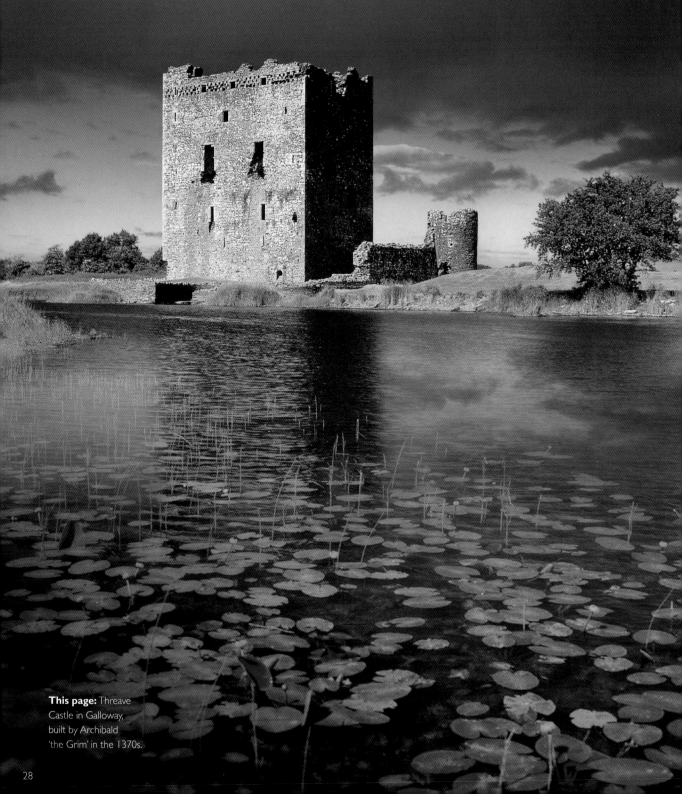

This page: Threave Castle in Galloway, built by Archibald 'the Grim' in the 1370s.

'Hush ye! Hush ye! Dinna fret ye!
The Black Douglas wilna get ye!'
Nursery rhyme

Below : A painted silk ceremonial standard associated the Douglases of Cavers.

Bottom: The Douglas crest badge. The French motto translates as, 'Never at the rear'.

THE STORY OF CLAN DOUGLAS

The Douglases are one of Lowland Scotland's greatest clans. They were forever putting the fear of death into the English, they blew hot and cold regarding loyalty to their own king, and they spent as much time fighting amongst themselves as they did against their foes. Their chiefs' by-names speak for themselves – 'the Hardy', 'the Grim' and 'the Gross' – and they bestrode not just Scotland but England and continental Europe as well. Following the death in battle of James, the 2nd Earl, the dynasty split in two, the senior line taking the name 'the Black Douglases' and the junior line 'the Red Douglases'.

THE 'BLACK' DOUGLASES

For sheer bloodthirstiness, the Black Douglases take some beating. From the time of their rise to power during the Wars of Independence in the early 14th century, through to the day they were brought down by James II in 1455, the Black Douglases were seldom far from the battlefield or the bloodfeud. Even their place of origin suggests darkness, for Douglas derives from *du glas*, 'black water'.

The Douglases were modest landowners in Douglasdale in the 12th and 13th centuries. But when Robert Bruce made his audacious bid for the crown of Scotland in 1306, the 19-year-old James of Douglas threw in his lot with him and was soon doing great service. He ejected the English from several major castles, including his own at Douglas. It took three attempts – but this was, after all, the man who advised Bruce about the spider's determination to build his web.

He led a brigade at the momentous Battle of Bannockburn in 1314, and thereafter took the fight to the English, raiding deep into the northern counties; he very nearly captured Edward II and his queen, Isabella, in Yorkshire in 1319. To the English, the man with the jet-black hair and sallow skin was the Devil's spawn. Parents in England's northern counties, trying to get their frightened children off to sleep, would whisper verses to them about the Black Douglas, hoping to ward off the fear they themselves must have felt.

To the Scots, the Black Douglas became 'the Good Sir James of Douglas', Bruce's right-hand man 'mair fell [fierce] than was ony devill in hell'. James was richly rewarded for his loyalty, receiving a vast estate of lordships stretching across the southern uplands.

The warrior skills of the Good Sir James passed down through the generations. James's third cousin, William, recaptured mighty Edinburgh Castle for David II, Bruce's son, and booted the English out of Liddesdale, 'the bloodiest valley in Britain', earning the by-name 'the Knight of Liddesdale'. James's nephew, William, 1st Earl of Douglas, came into his inheritance by killing his own godfather, the same Knight of Liddesdale.

This picture: The magnificent ruins of Tantallon Castle at the mouth of the Firth of Forth, built in the 1350s by William, 1st Earl of Douglas.

William's son James, 2nd Earl of Douglas, was killed early on in the Battle of Otterburn against Henry 'Hotspur' Percy in 1388, yet he still contrived to win the day. Archibald the Grim, 3rd Earl and illegitimate son of the Good Sir James, wielded a sword so big that it was said no other man could lift it. He earned his nickname 'on account of his countenance in warfare against the English'.

Archibald's son, the 4th Earl, was feted across Europe for his fighting qualities, rising to become Duke of Touraine and Lieutenant-General of France in 1424. Never before in French history had such an honour been bestowed on a foreign nobleman.

The year 1424 marked the peak of Black Douglas power. Following the 4th Earl's death fighting the English at the Battle of Verneuil, the clan went into a tailspin. The 5th Earl died of the plague, the 6th Earl was summarily executed in Edinburgh Castle following the so-called 'Black Dinner' he received therein, and the 8th Earl was killed 12 years later at the king's own hand at Stirling Castle. Only the formidable bulk and equally formidable political skills of the 7th Earl, James 'the Gross', temporarily stemmed the tide.

They were eventually overwhelmed in 1455, when James II went on the offensive against his over-mighty subjects, taking castle after Black Douglas castle, until only mighty Threave was holding out. By the time the king arrived at the siege, the rump of the Black Douglas forces had been routed at Arkinholm, in the eastern Borders. By then the 9th Earl of Douglas was in hiding in England. He slunk back in 1484 but was captured at Lochmaben and imprisoned. The day he died in his cell at Lindores Abbey in 1488 was the day the Black Douglases' 150-year grip on power came to its end.

Right: The Douglas arms, with Bruce's 'bludy hert' at their centre.

DID YOU KNOW...

At the centre of the Douglas arms lies a heart. It recalls the exploits of the Good Sir James following Bruce's death in 1329. When Bruce, on his death-bed, asked his good friend to carry his heart on crusade, James did not hesitate. The following year, he died as he had lived, fighting in battle — this time against the Moors in far-off Spain, Bruce's heart in its casket around his neck. His nephew, William, the 1st Earl, adopted the 'bludy hert' soon after its return to Scotland with the body of 'the Black Douglas'.

THE RED DOUGLASES

By comparison, the Red Douglases were tame. No by-names for them to compare with 'Grim' and 'Gross'. Only one was bestowed – 'Bell-the-Cat', implying that Archibald, 5th Earl of Angus, was a mere mouse.

But everything is relative. The Red Douglases may not have reached the heights – or depths – of devilish cunning of their Black kinsmen, but they had almost as many skeletons in their cupboards.

The origins of the Red Douglases resemble a medieval soap opera. William, 1st Earl of Douglas, was married to Margaret, sister of the Earl of Mar, who bore him a son, James. But Earl William also took a mistress, his brother-in-law's widow, Margaret, Countess of Angus, and she too bore him a son, George. Upon Earl William's death in 1384 , James succeeded as 2nd Earl. But when he too died four years later, without legitimate heir, the dynastic succession was thrown into confusion. Seizing her chance, Countess Margaret resigned her Earldom of Angus in favour of George, thus splitting the house of Douglas in two. The senior line passed to Archibald the Grim, son of the Black Douglas, whence the Black Douglases. George founded the junior line, the Red Douglases. Both houses were now headed by illegitimate offspring – but this was Clan Douglas after all.

The Red Douglases may have lacked the warrior skills of their senior kinsmen, but they made up for it in devious cunning. They wasted no time in getting their own back on their Black kinsmen, worming their way into the confidence of the Stewart kings and leading James II's army at Arkinholm. They reaped rich rewards for their pains, and following the king's death at the siege of Roxburgh in 1460, George, 4th Earl of Angus, was accorded the privilege of placing the crown on little James III's head in the hallowed surroundings of Kelso Abbey.

Right: A portrait of the Italian School, thought to show Archibald, 4th Earl of Douglas and Duke of Touraine.

THE DOUGLASES

c.1160	**William, son of Erkenbald** settles in Douglasdale.
1307	**James 'of Douglas'** joins Robert Bruce. Called the 'Black Douglas' because of his black hair.
1314	**James** recaptures Roxburgh, then leads a **brigade at Bannockburn.**
1330	**James** killed in Spain, carrying Bruce's heart to the Holy Land.
1342	James's cousin, **William**, made Lord of Dalkeith and Liddesdale by David II. Known as 'the Knight of Liddesdale'.
1358	James's nephew, **William**, created Earl of Douglas by David II. Builds Tantallon Castle.
1362	James's illegitimate son, **Archibald 'the Grim'**, rebuilds Bothwell Castle.
1369	**Archibald** created Lord of Galloway by David II. Builds Threave Castle.
1389	**George**, son of 1st Earl's widow, becomes Earl of Angus and first 'Red' Douglas, based at Tantallon.
1452	**William, 8th Earl of Douglas**, killed by James II in Stirling Castle.
1455	**James II** defeats Black Douglases at Arkinholm and captures Threave, their last castle.
1514	**Archibald, 6th Earl of Angus**, marries James IV's widow, Margaret Tudor.
1528	**James V** besieges Tantallon.
1567	**William of Lochleven**, receives Mary Queen of Scots as his prisoner. **James, 4th Earl of Morton**, presides over her abdication there.
1572	**Morton** becomes regent, and retakes Edinburgh Castle for James VI (1573).
1581	**Morton** executed for his part in Lord Darnley's murder.
1633	**William, Viscount Drumlanrig**, created Earl of Queensberry by Charles I.
1684	**William, 3rd Earl**, made Duke of Queensberry by Charles II. Builds Drumlanrig Castle.

Above and right: Two details from a double portrait of Archibald, 6th Earl of Douglas and his wife Margaret Tudor.

It was George's son Archibald, the 5th Earl, who earned the by-name 'Bell-the-Cat', awarded when he hanged seven of James III's 'low-born familiars' from Lauder Bridge in 1482. A contemporary wrote: 'the mice [i.e. the aristocracy] would fain hang a bell around the cat [King James] that preyed on them, but which mouse was to bell the cat?' Step forward Archibald Douglas.

Archibald also set the Red Douglases on a pro-English course. In 1491, he entered into a treasonable pact with Henry VII, and was only brought back into line when James IV besieged his castle at Tantallon. His grandson, the 6th Earl, pursued the same road – despite losing his father at Flodden in 1513. He even married Margaret Tudor, Henry VII's daughter and James IV's widow.

There were setbacks on the way. In 1528 Archibald temporarily lost use of mighty Tantallon following a devastating artillery bombardment by James V, and in 1544 he learned that the English had ransacked his ancestors' tombs in Melrose Abbey, compelling him to change sides briefly. He led his countrymen into battle twice against the 'Auld Enemy', winning one (Ancrum Moor, 1545) and losing the other (Pinkie, 1547).

Right: A statue of James Douglas, Earl of Angus, who raised the Cameronian Regiment at Douglas Castle, Lanarkshire, in 1689.

Ultimately, his family prospered. In 1567, Mary Queen of Scots was forced to abdicate to his kinsman, James, 4th Earl of Morton, in another Douglas castle, Lochleven. Morton subsequently became Regent, and retook Edinburgh Castle for Mary's son, James VI. Alas, Regent Morton didn't live long thereafter. In 1581, he was executed on 'the Maiden', Edinburgh's guillotine, for his part in the murder of Darnley, Mary's second husband.

Thereafter, the Red Douglas story is one of loyalty to the Protestant throne. In 1689, following James VII & II's flight into exile, James, Earl of Angus, raised the Cameronian Regiment in the grounds of Douglas Castle to fight for the Protestant Prince William of Orange. His men were soon in action, beating off a Jacobite assault on Dunkeld following the defeat at Killiecrankie.

It was fitting, therefore, that a Douglas should preside over the Act of Union of 1707 that created the United Kingdom and secured the Protestant succession. James, 2nd Duke of Queensberry, Queen Anne's Scottish Commissioner, astutely engineered the bill through a raucous Parliament, earning opprobrium and plaudits in equal measure. Thirty-eight years later, Prince Charles Edward Stuart, James VII & II's grandson, spent Christmas at Queensberry's seat of Drumlanrig on his retreat from Derby. Needless to say he had not been invited.

Above: Bothwell Castle in South Lanarkshire, which passed into Douglas hands in 1362, when Archibald 'the Grim' married Lady Joanna of Moray.

THE BLACK DOUGLAS CASTLES

Black Douglas castles are much like the Black Douglases themselves – grim and forbidding. Tantallon, Threave and the rest are the visible manifestations of the mighty lords who once dwelt within. Even today, in their ruined states, they overawe.

Of their ancestral seat, Douglas, nothing survives. It must have been the equal of the rest, for it took the Black Douglas three attempts to recapture it in 1307. It is said he ultimately caught its English garrison off-guard whilst they were at prayer. He had them all slaughtered and dumped in the cellars, then set fire to the place, hence the castle's nickname 'Douglas's Larder'. It was rebuilt after the Wars of Independence, but by then the Black Douglases had largely turned their backs on the 'black water' in Upper Clydesdale and built new castles elsewhere. But Douglas remained forever in their hearts, and St Bride's Kirk there became their mausoleum. The effigy of the Good Sir James and other Black Douglases can still be admired there today.

The castle that replaced Douglas as the clan's chief seat was mighty Tantallon, rising spectacularly from a rocky promontory beside the Firth of Forth. The Good Sir James's nephew, William, built it in the 1350s to celebrate his becoming Earl of Douglas. The awesome red sandstone curtain wall drawn across the neck of the headland has a somewhat careworn appearance now, having been battered not only by cannon but by the winds that are as much a part of that exposed spot as the rugged cliffs themselves, but it is still awe-inspiring. High above his front door, Earl William placed a stone plaque with the 'bludy hert' carved thereon; in its prime that heart would have been painted blood red.

Around the time Earl William was moving into Tantallon, his cousin Archibald the Grim was also relocating. In 1362 he married Lady Joanna of Moray, whose family seat was Bothwell Castle, beside a bend in the River Clyde a few miles south of Glasgow. The monumentally impressive 13th-century castle had taken a real pounding in the Wars of Independence and it fell to Archibald to rebuild it. He abandoned the great 13th-century round tower badly damaged in the wars, and in its stead built a rectangular tower at the far end of the sprawling castle precinct. Beside it his son, Archibald, Duke of Touraine, built an equally impressive great hall. The hall is still there, but the Grim's great tower collapsed long ago. To envisage what it looked like, we need only visit the other great castle that Archibald the Grim built – Threave.

Right: An early 14th-century seal matrix found at Threave. It belonged to Princess Margaret, daughter of Robert III and wife of Archibald, 4th Earl of Douglas. On the right is the seal's impression in wax, featuring Douglas hearts and royal lions.

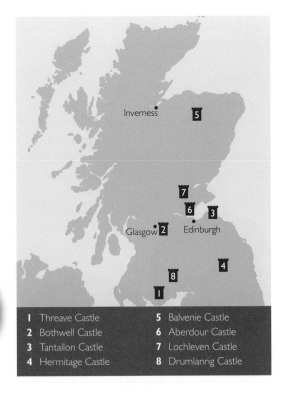

1	Threave Castle	5	Balvenie Castle
2	Bothwell Castle	6	Aberdour Castle
3	Tantallon Castle	7	Lochleven Castle
4	Hermitage Castle	8	Drumlanrig Castle

Above: Aberdour Castle in Fife, a more picturesque building than most Douglas strongholds.

Right: Artist's impression of the artillerymen at Threave, who held James II's forces at bay for three months in 1455.

Archibald built Threave on becoming Lord of Galloway in 1369. The island in the River Dee was once crowded with buildings, but all that remains now is his huge tower house, whose thick walls rise to almost 30m high, the equivalent of a 10-storey block of flats. Externally it appears closed-up and grim, just like its builder. Inside were five floors providing all the private accommodation a man near the top of the social ladder needed: a basement with a well and prison; a kitchen and common hall; Archibald's own hall; his two-roomed private apartment; and a fighting floor with battlements. Threave was a trend-setter, helping establish a new style of lordly residence that Scots would take to their hearts. Earl William, Archibald's cousin, followed suit, building formidable tower houses at Newark, in the Ettrick Forest, and Hermitage, in Liddesdale.

Threave's great tower is not its only architectural innovation. Wrapped around its base is an artillery work built around 1450, around the time the 8th Earl of Douglas was preparing for his showdown with James II. Gunpowdered artillery was then still in the experimental stage, and some have cast doubt on its dating,

believing Scotland couldn't possibly have anything so innovative. But this is to ignore the outstanding military pedigree of the Black Douglases. Earl William's uncle, the 4th Earl, was none other than Lieutenant-General of France, feted across Europe as one of the finest warriors of his day. That artillery defence was probably the chief obstacle to James II winning Threave by might in 1455. After a siege lasting more than three months, during which he unleashed his latest gun on the stronghold, James finally had to resort to bribing the garrison into surrender.

Left: Wooden bowls found at Threave. They are branded on the underside with the Douglas heart.

DID YOU KNOW…

In 1976, archaeologists were excavating in the silted-up harbour at Threave Castle. Among the many artefacts discovered – including a barrel full of gunstones, ivory chess-pieces and children's leather shoes with wee holes in the soles – were wooden bowls and plates, broken or burned and thrown away. Branded into their undersides was the 'bludy hert', the Douglases' logo.

THE RED DOUGLAS CASTLES

When Clan Douglas split into two in 1388, George, Earl of Angus, fell heir to mighty Tantallon. Tantallon remained the Red Douglases' chief seat until a combination of old age and artillery bombardment took their toll. Tantallon served the Red earls well, given their predilection for political intrigue. Both Bell-the-Cat and his grandson, the 6th Earl, successfully holed up therein, despite artillery sieges by James IV (1491) and James V (1528).

It was the castle's third recorded siege, by Cromwell in 1651, that brought about its end. The devastation wrought by the English guns is still plain to see, in the shattered Douglas and East Towers. An inventory of the castle's contents, made soon afterwards, confirms that it had long been abandoned by its noble residents – the Douglas Tower, for example, could only boast 'ane ald bedstead' and 'an ald table'.

By 1651, the Red Douglases were more comfortably residing at Bothwell and Douglas, castles they acquired following the overthrow of their Black kinsmen in 1455. Both were subsequently abandoned in favour of more 'modern' country houses, neither of which has survived.

OTHER DOUGLAS CASTLES

Several cadets of the Black Douglases sprang up and continued to prosper long after the demise of the senior line. They included the Douglases of Dalkeith (later Earls of Morton) and Drumlanrig. Both left behind some fine castles.

The Douglases of Dalkeith were descended from William, the Knight of Liddesdale. In 1458 James II elevated the 3rd Lord Dalkeith to the earldom of Morton as a reward for helping overthrow the Black Douglases. In addition to Dalkeith, they had estates in West Lothian (Morton), Fife (Aberdour and Lochleven) and Peeblesshire (Drochil).

Nothing remains of Dalkeith Castle, but the other residences remain as ruins. Aberdour, their second home, looks nothing like a Black Douglas castle. It has a welcoming demeanour and picturesque architectural details. The surrounding terraced gardens were probably contributed by Regent Morton, the 4th Earl, who had a penchant for gardening, when he wasn't busy plotting Darnley's murder, besieging Edinburgh Castle, or receiving his queen's abdication.

The Douglases of Drumlanrig, in Dumfriesshire, were descended from an illegitimate son of the 2nd Earl, but medieval Drumlanrig is no more. The present Baroque confection, completed in the 1690s for the 1st Duke of Queensberry, was a profound departure from the old, familiar castles. Apparently the duke spent just one night there before returning to his previous residence, Sanquhar Castle. The chief of Clan Douglas clearly felt more at home behind his stone shield. His forebear, the Black Douglas, would have been proud of him.

Below: Drumlanrig Castle, Dumfriesshire, completed in the 1690s. Its Baroque splendour proved too elaborate for William Douglas, 1st Duke of Queensberry.

Right: James Douglas, 4th Earl of Morton, who received Mary Queen of Scots' abdication at Lochleven Castle.

CLAN
FRASER

'As lang as there's a Cock o' the North, there'll be a Fraser in Philorth.'

Traditional saying

Opposite: Cairnbulg Castle, near Fraserburgh, built in the 1370s as chief seat of the Frasers of Philorth.

Below: The Fraser crest badge. The French motto translates as, 'I am ready'.

Right: Yew, the plant badge of the Frasers.

THE STORY OF CLAN FRASER

The Frasers seem as Highland as malt whisky, yet their story begins in the Scottish Borders. They were not the only ones to make the journey, for their famous Highland neighbours, the Chisholms and the Gordons, did so too. The Frasers came to Scotland in the 12th century, but from where is a mystery; La Frézelière, in Anjou's Loire Valley, seems likely, and would explain the other version of their surname – Frisell. Numerous Scottish surnames derive from their French origins, including other notable Border families, such as Hay (from La Haye-Bellefonds, near Saint-Lô), and, most famously, Bruce (Brus, now Brix, near Cherbourg).

The first Fraser on record was Simon, who granted an East Lothian church to Kelso Abbey around 1160. By 1200, the Frasers had become lords of Oliver (now Tweedsmuir), in Upper Tweeddale. Throughout the 13th century, they served as sheriffs of Peebles, and one of them, William, became Bishop of St Andrews. They also began to inch north, establishing a branch at Touch, near Stirling. Both branches were inevitably caught up in the Wars of Independence, but with very different outcomes.

Simon of Oliver initially stole the limelight, leading the Scots to unexpected victory at Roslin in 1303, for which Edward of England, 'Hammer of the Scots', never forgave him.

He was eventually captured in 1306, shortly after attending Robert Bruce's coronation, and taken to London, where he underwent a grisly execution. Edward had his body and his gallows burned, and his severed head displayed on a pike on London Bridge next to Wallace's. The lands of Simon 'the Patriot' passed through marriage to their fellow incomers, the Hays.

The Touch-Frasers, by contrast, went from strength to strength. Alexander attended King Robert's first parliament at St Andrews in 1309, fought at Bannockburn in 1314 and signed the famous Declaration of Arbroath in 1320. Bruce rewarded him with the hand in marriage of his sister, Lady Mary, the post of chamberlain, and extensive estates in lower Deeside, forfeited by the 'Black Comyn', erstwhile Earl of Buchan. Alas, Alexander and his brother Simon died at the hands of the English, on the battlefields of Dupplin and Halidon Hill respectively.

By 1400, the Frasers were fully established as Highlanders. Alexander's line acquired Philorth, in Buchan, through marriage. A cadet, the Frasers of Muchall-in-Mar, was created 50 years later. Simon's family, meanwhile, relocated to Lovat and the Aird, west and south of Inverness, and became so thoroughly imbued with Gaelic culture that they adopted the patronymic MacShimi, 'son of Simon'. One chief was so proud to be a Highlander that he had the bagpipes played not only at his wedding but at the consummation too!

Left: A 19th-century engraving of Castle Fraser by R. W. Billings.

Right: Simon Fraser, 'The Spider of Dounie', as caricatured by the great satirist William Hogarth.

THE FRASERS

c.1200	**Udard Fraser** becomes lord of Oliver through marriage.
1303	**Simon of Oliver** leads Scots to victory over English at Roslin.
1306	**Simon** executed in London and head put on spike beside Wallace's.
1316	Simon's cousin, **Alexander**, marries Mary, Robert Bruce's sister, and acquires lands in NE Scotland.
1367	**Hugh Fraser** acquires Lovat through marriage.
1375	Alexander's grandson, **Alexander**, acquires Philorth through marriage. Builds Philorth Castle (Cairnbulg Castle).
1454	**Thomas Fraser** acquires Muchall-in-Mar.
c.1460	**Hugh Fraser** created Lord Lovat.
1511	**Thomas, 2nd Lord Lovat**, builds Castle Dounie.
1544	**Around 300 Frasers** killed fighting MacDonalds at Battle of Blar-na-Leine.
c.1570	**Alexander, 8th of Philorth**, builds Kinnaird Head Castle. Michael, 6th of Muchall, begins Castle Fraser.
1613	**Alexander Fraser** forced to sell Philorth through bankruptcy.
1633	**Andrew, 7th of Muchalls**, created Lord Fraser by Charles I.
1699	**Simon** becomes 11th Lord Lovat and plays duplicitous game between government and Jacobites.
1746	**Around 250 Frasers** killed at Culloden. Simon executed (1747).
1757	**Simon's son** raises Fraser Highlanders to fight for Wolfe in Quebec.

They had aspirations to be lords in the heart of the Gaidhealtachd also, but in 1544 encountered the mighty MacDonalds in the bloodiest clan fight in history. The Battle of Blar-na-Leine, in the mountains above Loch Lochy, was fought out in such a heat that the clansmen had to strip off – hence *blar-na-leine*, 'field of shirts'. By the end of the day, 300 Frasers lay dead, including the clan chief and his son.

Meanwhile, their kinsmen at Philorth and Muchalls were living in comparative peace. They were sometimes obliged to go into battle – for example, turning out for Mary Queen of Scots against the mighty Gordons at Corrichie in 1562 – but their time was mostly spent more creatively. In the 1570s and 80s Alexander, 8th Lord of Philorth, transformed the fishing village of Faithlie into a new town, Fraserburgh. He built a new castle there, and would have built a university too had he not run into debt.

Around the same time, Michael, 6th of Muchalls, was creating a splendid new residence, Castle Fraser, near Inverurie. His son, Andrew, completed the work and was created Lord Fraser in 1633 by Charles I.

When Charles's son, James VII & II, was forced into exile in 1689, Andrew's descendant, Charles, 4th Lord Fraser, displayed his loyalty to the banished Stewarts by drinking His Majesty's health in public. He was fined £200 – a very substantial sum at that time. Undaunted, he battled on until the Jacobite Rising of 1715, when he was chased off an Aberdeenshire cliff by redcoats. It was the end of the line not just for him but for his line of Frasers.

If there was no doubting the loyalty of Fraser of Muchalls to the Jacobite cause, there was every reason to question that of his kinsman, Simon Fraser, 11th of Lovat. The man was forever switching allegiance, chiefly to advance his own ambition. So devious was he that contemporaries dubbed him 'the Fox' and 'the Spider of Dounie' (after his chief residence near Beauly). In 1716, for example, he was retaking Inverness Castle for George I; seven years later he was being belted Duke of Fraser by the exiled 'James VIII & III' (the Old Pretender).

His duplicity eventually undid him. By the time of Culloden he was a Jacobite once more – but only after Prince Charles Edward Stuart had beaten George II twice in battle – sending 250 clansmen to their deaths on that fateful day. The old Fox, fast approaching 80, fled into the mountains but was soon caught and sent to London. He was beheaded on Tower Hill in 1747, the last nobleman in Britain to be given that dubious honour. His son tried hard to retrieve the situation, raising a regiment to fight for king and country against the French in Quebec. The Fraser Highlanders were the first in a distinguished line of 'Fighting Frasers'.

Above: The 'Fighting Frasers' witness the death of General Wolfe at the Battle of Quebec in a painting by Benjamin West.

DID YOU KNOW...

Clan Fraser provides the first record of a Highland Games. In 1655, the Frasers held a tainchel (from the Gaelic word *timchioll*, meaning 'circuit') beside Loch a' Mhuillidh, in Strath Farrar. According to the local minister, the Reverend James Fraser, his clansmen exercised in 'jumping, arching, shooting, throwing the barr [perhaps an early version of today's hammer], the stone, and all manner of manly exercise imaginable'.

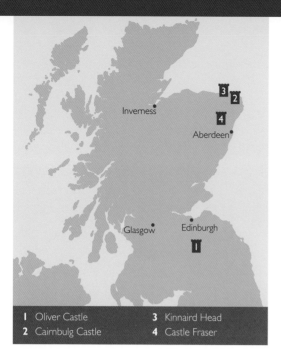

1 Oliver Castle	3 Kinnaird Head
2 Cairnbulg Castle	4 Castle Fraser

Right: Sir Alexander Fraser, 8th Lord of Philorth, who was forced to sell Cairnbulg, having funded the establishment of Fraserburgh.

CASTLES OF THE FRASERS

In the secluded upper reaches of the River Tweed, at a place now called Tweedsmuir but once known as Oliver, stands a pretty spired late-Victorian kirk. The kirk stands on a trim green mound that may well be the motte, or castle mound, on which Udard Fraser built his residence around 1200. That modest mound is all that survives as a testament to the Frasers of Oliver, or indeed to any of the Lowland Frasers, for their castles at Touch and elsewhere have all gone. Thankfully, the seats they subsequently built in the Highlands have stood the test of time far better. They are among the finest late-medieval castles in Scotland.

The impressive castle of Cairnbulg beside the Water of Philorth was built as the chief seat of the Frasers of Philorth, following the family's acquisition of the estate through marriage in 1375. It now stands a little inland from the chilly wastes of the North Sea, but when the Frasers arrived here the spot would have been hard by the beach. The original tower house, massive and high, was built for Alexander Fraser and his wife, Joanna Leslie, daughter of the 5th Earl of Ross. It still dominates a fascinating complex of buildings added by subsequent generations of Frasers of Philorth.

But in 1613 they were compelled to sell up, thanks to the debts run up by the 8th Lord investing in his new town, Fraserburgh. For the next 300 years the Frasers' ancient seat passed through various hands until the opportunity arose in 1934 to repurchase it. It remains the clan seat to this day.

An integral part of the 8th Lord's development of Fraserburgh was the construction of a second castle. It is not clear whether Kinnaird Head was intended to replace Cairnbulg or augment it. It too was centred on a lofty tower house, surrounded by ranges of buildings. Time has taken its toll on Kinnaird Head. More precisely, it was altered beyond recognition by the Northern Lighthouse Board who, in 1787, converted it into their first operating lighthouse. They gutted the interior and swept away the enveloping buildings – all except the enigmatic Wine Tower beside the cliff edge, which still features fine Fraser heraldic bosses on the top floor. According to legend, the laird had his daughter's lover manacled in a sea cave below this tower, so that he drowned at high tide. The distraught girl threw herself to her death.

Right: Castle Fraser, among the most impressive late-medieval buildings in NE Scotland.

Left: An architectural detail at Castle Fraser.

Below: Kinnaird Head, a fine tower house dramatically altered to become a lighthouse.

*'There, bound in cruel fetters, lies
the lover found and true;
No more to glad the maiden's eyes,
mo more to bless her view!'*

'The Ballad of the Wine Tower',
published in Pratt's Buchan (c. 1860)

Thanks to the skulduggery of Simon Fraser, the 'Spider of Dounie', during the Jacobite troubles, little remains of the medieval castles of the Frasers of Lovat. One crannog, or island stronghold, still stands in lonely Loch a' Mhuillidh, which may have served as a hunting lodge, and there are two 17th-century tower houses, at Dalcross and Moniack, both heavily restored and inhabited. Nothing at all survives of the Spider's chief seat, Castle Dounie, beside Beauly. 'Butcher' Cumberland, younger son of George II, made sure of that. After routing the Jacobites at Culloden, he sent in his redcoats to raze Dounie to the ground. From its ashes arose the phoenix that is Beaufort House, built in the 1880s for the restored Lovat chief.

Finally, there is Castle Fraser. Of all the fine late-medieval castles in NE Scotland, none can quite match it for sheer impressiveness.

For that we should thank Michael Fraser, 6th laird of Muchall, and his son Andrew, the 1st Lord Fraser. It was they who, during the reign of James VI (1567–1625), contracted two notable architectural families in NE Scotland, the Leipers and the Bells, to transform the 15th-century tower house of their forebears into the splendid castle complex we admire today. Centre stage stands the great seven-storey round tower with its imitation cannon water-spouts and parapet balustrade.

CLAN
GORDON

This page: Huntly Castle, Aberdeenshire. The 15th century castle was greatly improved in the 16th century by George Gordon, 4th Earl of Huntly and his grandson, George Gordon, 1st Marquis.

'A Gordon for me, a Gordon for me,
If ye're no' a Gordon ye're no use to me.'
Popular music-hall song by Robert Wilson

Left: Ivy, the plant badge
of the Gordons.

Below: The Gordon crest
badge. The motto translates
as, 'Remaining'.

THE STORY OF CLAN GORDON

The Gordons were the greatest clan in NE Scotland in the later Middle Ages, wielding power like kings. Their rise began in the 14th century, and reached its zenith 200 years later, under the 4th Earl of Huntly, 'Cock o' the North'. The Gordons rubbed shoulders with royalty and held high office. They were also renowned fighters, shedding their blood for sovereign and country 'at home and abroad, on the battlefield and on the scaffold', as James Taylor puts it in *The Great Historic Families of Scotland*. But they also indulged heavily in the 'bloodfeud', and many another clan suffered at their hands.

The clan's origins are obscure. The first on record is Richard de Gordon, who granted land on his Berwickshire estate to Kelso Abbey around 1160. We do not know where Richard's forebears hailed from. The suggestion that they originated in a Macedonian city called Gordonia is clearly fantasy. They may have been Norman incomers, invited to settle in Scotland by David I (1124–53), an origin they would have shared with the Frasers.

For 200 years, the de Gordons remained in Berwickshire. The fighting spirit for which they later became renowned was soon in evidence. Tradition tells of Adam de Gordon going on Crusade in 1270, and dying in north Africa. He was the first of the clan whose death on the battlefield is recorded; he was by no means the last.

By 1300 the Gordons had become embroiled in the Wars of Independence with England. Sir Adam Gordon remained loyal to King John Balliol until the latter's death in 1313, and only then joined Robert Bruce, around the time of Bannockburn. This was the defining moment in the clan's history, for Bruce gave Adam the rich estate of Strathbogie, in Aberdeenshire, forfeited by the treacherous Earl of Atholl, who had destroyed Bruce's supply camp at Cambuskenneth on the eve of Bannockburn. In 1320 Adam was entrusted to take the famous Declaration of Arbroath to Pope John XXII.

The Gordons did not enter fully into their northern inheritance until 1376. They did not entirely forsake their southern roots, continuing to hold Gordon, and establishing important branches elsewhere, such as the Gordons of Lochinvar, in Galloway, through Adam's second son, William. They also continued to lay down their lives on the battlefield. Adam himself fell at Halidon Hill (1333), and his descendants at Neville's Cross (1346), Otterburn (1388), and Homildon Hill (1402).

The death of the second Adam at Homildon brought to an end the male Gordon line. The family inheritance passed to his daughter Elizabeth. In 1408 she married Alexander Seton, descended from another Lowland family. The Gordon name could have passed into history, but it proved so potent that when Alexander was ennobled around 1437 he took the title Lord Gordon. When the 2nd Lord

Far left: Ruthven Barracks, near Aviemore, built following the 1715 Jacobite Rising on the site of a Gordon castle.

Left: Greenknowe Tower, built on the probable site of the first Gordon Castle.

became an earl around 1445 he chose to become Earl of Huntly, after a village on the Gordons' ancestral estate in Berwickshire. Shortly afterwards he changed his family name from Seton to Gordon. By 1450 the Gordons were well established in their NE fiefdom.

Loyalty to the Crown remained the Gordon watchword. The 1st Earl helped James II overcome the Black Douglases, the 2nd Earl fought for the enfeebled James III at Sauchieburn in 1488, and the 3rd Earl fought beside James IV at Flodden in 1513. They reaped further rewards, receiving Ruthven-in-Badenoch in 1451, and being appointed to high office in Church and State. Through bonds of manrent, the clan chief took the allegiance not only of his own kindred but of most of the leading Highland families, among them Cameron of Lochiel, Drummond of Blair, Fraser of Lovat, Grant of Freuchie and MacLeod of Lewis.

Such was Clan Gordon's power that they became closely linked to royalty. In 1459 the 2nd Earl married James I's daughter, Annabella, so introducing Royal Stewart blood into Gordon veins. In 1496, the 2nd Earl's daughter, Catherine, wed Perkin Warbeck, pretender to the English throne during the Wars of the Roses – and became known as 'The White Rose of Scotland'.

But it was the 4th Earl who raised the family to the dizzy heights. Courtesy of his mother, James IV's illegitimate daughter, young George grew up at the royal court with James V. Their close friendship elevated George to the office

of chancellor, and brought him untold riches. His wealth earned him his soubriquet 'Cock o' the North'; it also brought about his downfall.

In 1556 Queen Marie de Guise visited Earl George at Huntly Castle. She was taken aback by her loyal subject's lavish hospitality. A 1,000-strong guard of honour welcomed her, and throughout her visit relays of hunters and fowlers, stalking in the hills and woods around, daily forwarded fresh game to the castle. After a few days, she offered to depart, to relieve the burden on her host. The earl wouldn't hear of it, and reassured her by showing her around his cavernous vaults, stuffed with provisions. At this, Marie's French ambassador urged her to 'clip the wings' of the Cock o' the North.

The opportunity to do so came soon afterwards, during the reign of Marie's daughter, Mary Queen of Scots. The pretext was the earl's continued adherence to Catholicism, despite the Protestant Reformation of 1560 and Scotland's break with Rome. Political necessity persuaded Mary to move against the earl. So it was that in October 1562 the royal army confronted him at Corrichie, near Huntly. It seems the corpulent earl fell from his horse and was suffocated by his own armour. Nevertheless, his embalmed corpse was taken to Edinburgh, tried and found guilty. The Cock o' the North's wings had been thoroughly clipped.

Somehow the Gordons survived and thrived, despite their continuing adherence to Rome. The 5th Earl was restored to his lands and titles, and died at Huntly in 1576 on the football field not the battlefield.

The 6th Earl should have shared a fate similar to his grandfather, given his involvement in a string of treasonable acts, including the bizarre 'Spanish Blanks' plot of 1592, a conspiracy with Catholic Spain. These tried the patience of his close friend James VI, who eventually had no option but to take action. By 1594, the earl was in exile – but not for long. Within three years he was home, and winning over James, who made him Marquis of Huntly. The redoubtable marquis lived to the age of 73. In 1636 he was buried in Elgin Cathedral, mausoleum of his forebears; his funeral was the final snub to Protestantism, conducted as it was according to the Catholic rite.

His passing effectively ended Gordon dominance in the north. They continued to enjoy a certain influence in the region, but never again on the scale enjoyed by the Cock o' the North. They continued to fly the flag for Rome, and supported the Royal Stewarts. In 1649, the 2nd Marquis lost his head on the scaffold for Charles I. The 4th Marquis, created Duke of Gordon in 1684 by Charles II, stoutly defended Edinburgh Castle against the Protestant King William of Orange in 1689–90, during the first Jacobite Rising.

During the final Jacobite Rising, the 2nd Duke's widow laid out a breakfast for Prince Charles Edward Stuart as he passed by her Lowland home in 1745, on his march south. But the bloody encounter at Culloden the following year ended all hope of returning a Catholic sovereign to the throne. By 1780, a son of the 3rd Duke was leading the famous 'No Popery' riots in London, and 14 years later the 4th Duke raised the Gordon Highlanders to fight for George III. The 4th Earl and 1st Marquis would have turned in their graves at the news.

Right: Detail from a medieval painting of the Battle of Otterburn, where John Gordon was killed in 1388.

THE GORDONS

c.1160	**Richard de Gordon** grants land in Berwickshire to Kelso Abbey.
1313	**Sir Adam Gordon** joins King Robert Bruce.
1320	**Adam** takes Declaration of Arbroath to Pope, and is rewarded by Bruce with Strathbogie.
1333	Adam's second son, **William**, founds the Gordons of Lochinvar.
1408	Adam's great-great granddaughter, **Elizabeth**, marries **Alexander Seton**.
c.1437	**Alexander** created Lord Gordon by James I.
c.1445	**Alexander, 2nd Lord**, created Earl of Huntly by James II.
c.1457	**1st Earl** changes family name from Seton to Gordon.
1459	**George, 2nd Earl**, marries **Annabella**, daughter of James I. Their third son, **William**, founds Gordons of Gight.
1496	George's daughter, **Catherine**, marries **Perkin Warbeck**, pretender to the English throne.
1506	**Alexander, 3rd Earl**, renames Strathbogie as Huntly.
1556	**Marie de Guise** visits 4th Earl and is aghast at Huntly's opulence.
1562	**4th Earl** dies at Corrichie fighting Mary Queen of Scots' army.
1594	**George, 6th Earl**, flees to France after exposure of a plot to depose James VI. Huntly Castle partially destroyed.
1599	**6th Earl** belted Marquis of Huntly by James VI. Rebuilds Huntly.
1649	**George, 2nd Marquis**, executed for supporting Charles I.
1684	**4th Marquis** created Duke of Gordon by Charles II.

DID YOU KNOW...

In the early 18th century, one of the staunchest supporters of the 'Old Pretender' was John Gordon, laird of Glenbuchat, in Strathdon. He is said to have given George II nightmares, from which the king would awake, shouting in his broken English: 'De gread Glenbogged is goming!'

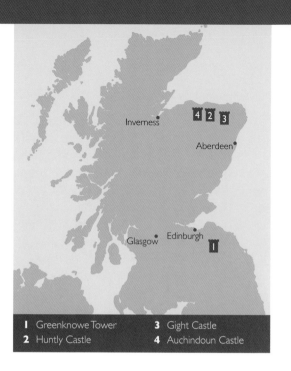

1 Greenknowe Tower   3 Gight Castle
2 Huntly Castle   4 Auchindoun Castle

CASTLES OF THE GORDONS

In the heart of the parish of Gordon, in Berwickshire, stands Greenknowe Tower. This pretty, late-16th-century tower house has no direct connection with Clan Gordon, but the grassy knoll it graces may well be the mound on which the first Gordon chiefs built their castle in the 12th century, and where they resided for their first 200 years on Scottish soil.

Another fine late-medieval castle stands 130 miles (210km) to the north of Greenknowe as the crow flies, at the place where the River Bogie rushes into the River Deveron. Huntly Castle also rises up from a grassy knoll, but here the roles are reversed, for the grassy knoll was built by an Earl of Fife in the 12th century, whereas the imposing stone castle is the work of the Gordons. In 1506, the Gordons changed the name of their new residence from Strathbogie to Huntly; tangible links to their southern roots were clearly important to this great northern clan.

Huntly is a noble ruin in a beautiful setting, remarkable both for the splendour of its architecture and for its stirring history. Only the foundations of the Gordons' original tower house now remain. James VI had it blown up in 1594, during one of his many spats with his drinking companion, the 6th Earl and 1st Marquis. Thankfully, the king refrained from destroying the adjacent palace begun in the 15th century and substantially upgraded by the powerful 4th Earl in the 1550s. It was here in 1556 that the Cock o' the North entertained James's grandmother Queen Marie in such fine style.

Another visitor, Sir Thomas Randolph, the English Ambassador, wrote: 'His house is best furnished of any I have seen in this country. His cheer is marvellous great.' An inventory of its contents, taken shortly after the earl's death in 1562, certainly presents an impressive picture of wealth and splendour. Among the rich tapestries and the four-poster beds hung with the finest damask were found the treasures of Aberdeen Cathedral, which had been handed to the pro-Catholic earl in 1559 to preserve them from the 'cleansings' of the Protestant Reformers.

The 6th Earl, not to be outdone, greatly embellished the palace at Huntly to celebrate his elevation to the marquisate in 1599. The stately row of oriel windows with their heraldic inscription, the grand entrance

doorway with its stunning armorial frontispiece, and the exquisitely-carved mantelpieces within presented one of the most splendid architectural sights of their day – and they still do.

The 1st Marquis was a prodigious builder of fine architecture and a creator of surrounding attractive landscapes. As well as embellishing Huntly, he built new country houses at Aboyne and Plewlands (which he renamed Gordonstoun), rebuilt the castle at Ruthven-in-Badenoch, and repaired his town houses in Elgin and Aberdeen. These have either vanished without trace, or been subsequently altered out of all recognition. However, the ghostly ruin of another of his creations still stands on the summit of the Braes o'Gight, overlooking the River Ythan, near Fyvie.

Gight was built by a son of the 2nd Earl in the 1450s but greatly enlarged and given a garden by the 1st Marquis. It seems to have been the preferred residence of his countess Henrietta, whom he married in hallowed Holyrood Abbey in 1588. But in 1592, at Gight, the countess carried out a most unhallowed act of violence against the chief of Clan Macintosh. He was there attempting to atone for his part in burning the Gordon stronghold at Auchindoun, in Glen Fiddich, during a particularly violent feud between the Gordons and the Forbeses. Her husband would have had him beheaded, she told him, but in his absence she, being altogether more merciful, would spare him. Macintosh responded by feigning willingness to submit to that humiliation and laid his head on a block used to butcher bullocks. Unable to resist the temptation, the countess had her cook part Macintosh's head from his body. The gaunt ruin of Gight recovered its reputation,

and is now better remembered as the home of Catherine Gordon, Lord Byron's mother.

Castles of the numerous branches of Clan Gordon can still be found across NE Scotland. Most exist as picturesque ruins in the landscape – none more dramatic than lonely Auchindoun, the home of the infamous Edom (Adam) o' Gordon. Edom earned lasting notoriety in 1571. During a long-running feud with Clan Forbes, he crossed over the mountains and descended on the tower of Forbes of Towie at Corgarff, in Strathdon. The laird was away, but his wife Margaret was at home and refused him entry. So he savagely set fire to the castle, murdering Margaret and the other 23 people in the tower. The massacre is remembered in the old ballad *Edom o' Gordon*:

'But when the lady saw the fire
Come flaming owre her head,
She wept and kiss'd her children twain,
Says, 'Bairns, we been but dead.'

DID YOU KNOW...

In 1562, following the death of the 4th Earl, royal courtiers drew up an inventory of the contents of Huntly Castle. Among the treasures, they discovered a silk tent, in which Edward II of England was said to have spent the night before his defeat at Bannockburn on 24 June 1314.

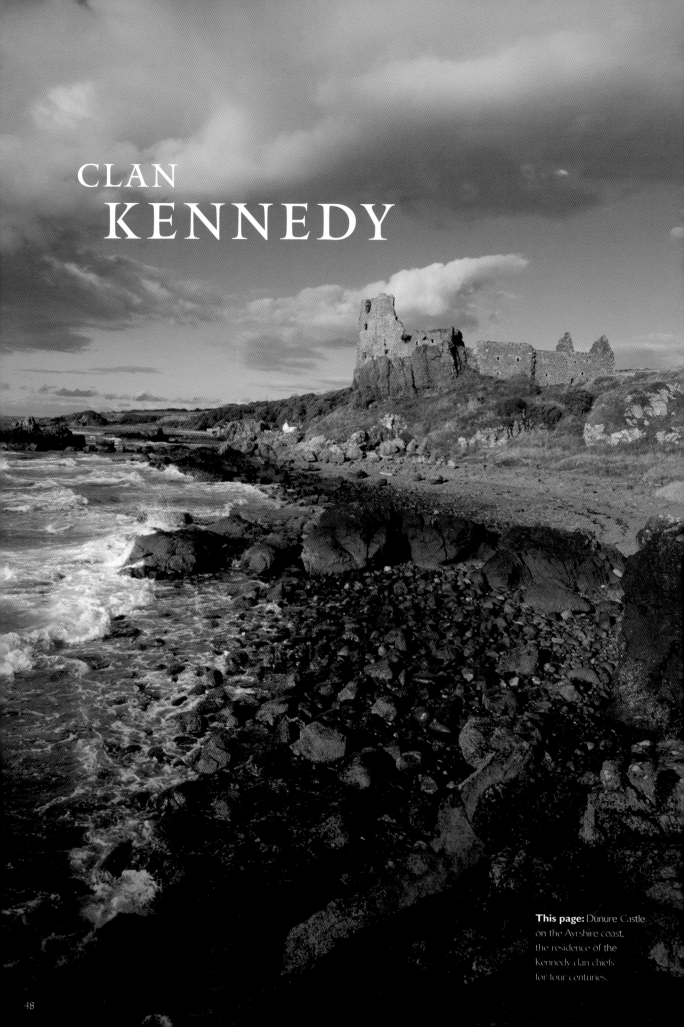

CLAN
KENNEDY

This page: Dunure Castle on the Ayrshire coast, the residence of the Kennedy clan chiefs for four centuries.

'Twixt Wigtoune and the toune o Aire
And laigh doun by the Cruves o Cree,
You shall not gett a lodging there
Except ye court a Kennedy!'

An old saying recorded in the 17th century

Left: Oak, the plant badge of the Kennedys.

Below: The Kennedy crest badge. The French motto translates as, 'Consider the end'.

THE STORY OF CLAN KENNEDY

The Kennedys are one of the great clans of SW Scotland. They emerged from the shadows of the crumbling Celtic province of Galloway in the 12th century to put their stamp on Carrick, in the NW of that ancient lordship.

Their power stemmed from their kinsman Duncan fitzGilbert. Grandson of the great Fergus of Galloway, he was made Lord, then Earl, of Carrick by William I. His son, Neil, died around 1256 without male heir, but he had made provision for his succession. His earldom was entrusted to his daughter Marjorie, but he passed the chieftaincy – and with it responsibility for leading his clansmen into battle – to his nephew Roland of Carrick. That is how the Kennedys are said to have acquired their surname, from the Gaelic *ceann-cinnidh*, meaning 'chief of kin'.

The Kennedy chiefs lived at Dunure Castle, a few miles up the coast from Turnberry Castle, the principal residence of the earls. Following Earl Neil's death, Countess Marjorie continued to reside there. She brought the place enduring fame when, around 1272, she kidnapped the handsome young Robert Bruce, Lord of Annandale, and dragged him back to Turnberry, where they married. Their first child, Robert Bruce, the future king, was born there shortly afterwards. From then on the Earldom of Carrick was held by the Bruces. At the momentous Battle of Bannockburn in 1314, the 'men of Carrick', under their chief, Gilbert Kennedy, formed part of Bruce's brigade.

Fighting was evidently in the Kennedys' blood. Hugh Kennedy of Ardstinchar led the Scots who helped Joan of Arc secure Orleans from the English in 1429. Another chief, David, fell alongside King James IV on the battlefield of Flodden in 1513. Just four years earlier James had belted him Earl of Cassillis – the name comes from an estate close to Maybole where, in 1373, John Kennedy of Dunure had established a collegiate church in which he and his heirs would be buried.

During the remainder of the 16th century, every one of David's three successors, all named Gilbert, met a violent end. The 2nd Earl was killed in Prestwick in 1527 following an altercation with Hugh Campbell of Loudon. The 3rd Earl died mysteriously in Dieppe, probably by poisoning; and the 4th Earl in 1576 after falling from his horse. This last Gilbert is better remembered, however, for welcoming two honoured guests to his stronghold at Dunure, in very different circumstances. In August 1563 he hosted Mary Queen of Scots during her royal progress in the area, but in August 1569 he roasted the Abbot of Crossraguel alive in an attempt to get him to sign over the abbey estates; apparently it took just two turns of the spit for the cleric to oblige!

The Kennedys weren't always so malevolently disposed towards the Church. James Kennedy, brother of the 1st Lord, became Bishop of

Far left: Magnificent Culzean Castle, built in the 18th century for the Kennedy earls of Cassillis.

Left: Thomas Kennedy, 9th Earl of Cassillis, who gained the title in 1762.

Below: John Kennedy, 7th Earl of Cassillis, who made a modest marriage to a London grocer's daughter.

Below, right: The towered gatehouse at Crossraguel Abbey, built by Abbot William Kennedy around 1525.

THE KENNEDYS

1186	**Duncan fitzGilbert** made Lord of Carrick by William I.
c.1225	**Duncan** created Earl of Carrick by Alexander II. Founds Crossraguel Abbey.
c.1256	**Neil, 2nd Earl** leaves earldom to daughter Marjorie, but proclaims his kinsman, Roland, chief of Clan Kennedy.
c.1272	**Marjorie** kidnaps and marries **Robert Bruce** the elder, who becomes new earl of Carrick.
1274	**Robert (later King Robert I)** born in Turnberry Castle 1274.
1314	**'The men of Carrick'** fight for Bruce at Bannockburn.
1372	**John Kennedy of Dunure** confirmed as chief. Founds collegiate church at Maybole.
1450	**James Kennedy**, Bishop of St Andrews, founds St Salvator's College.
1457	**Gilbert** created 1st Lord Kennedy by James II.
1509	**Donald, 3rd Lord**, created Earl of Cassillis by James IV.
1513	**Donald** killed at Flodden.
c.1525	**Abbot William Kennedy** builds new residence at Crossraguel.
1569	**Gilbert, 4th Earl**, roasts abbot of Crossraguel alive in Dunure.
1772	**Thomas, 9th Earl**, begins Culzean Castle.
1831	**Archibald**, 12th Earl, becomes Marquis of Ailsa.

St Andrews, and thus the leading cleric in the realm, in 1440. He founded St Salvator's College there in 1450, where he was laid to rest in 1465. A brother of the 2nd Earl, William, became abbot of Crossraguel in 1520 and built himself a fine new residence at the Abbey. His nephew, Quentin, who succeeded him, probably wrote his anti-Reformist bestseller, *Compendious Tractive*, there in 1558.

Subsequent centuries were relatively uneventful by Kennedy standards. Succeeding Earls of Cassillis all managed to die peacefully in their beds. John, the 7th Earl, even married a grocer's daughter from London in 1698 and died not in his native Carrick, but in leafy Surrey.

DID YOU KNOW...

In the 16th century a particularly troublesome band of Kennedys was forced to flee Ayrshire. They ended up in distant Lochaber, where they attached themselves to the MacDonalds of Glengarry and became known as Clan Ualraig (Ulrick). Ostensibly blacksmiths, they continued to indulge their passion for contract killing and arson.

CASTLES OF THE KENNEDYS

The coastline of Ayshire is studded with castles clinging to the cliff edges. Three stand barely six miles (10km) apart, between Ayr and Girvan, almost within sight of each other. And all three – Turnberry, Dunure and Culzean – are pivotal to the story of Clan Kennedy.

Turnberry was the most important in medieval times, though little can be made out today beneath the lighthouse that now occupies the site. The best indication that this is the probable birthplace of the great King Robert Bruce is the name of the ninth hole on the adjacent golf course – Bruce's Castle.

Turnberry is not strictly a Kennedy castle. Surnames were just coming into fashion in the late 12th century when Duncan fitzGilbert became 1st Lord of Carrick, then its 1st Earl, and built the castle. His son Neil was responsible for creating the Kennedy name before his death in 1256, when he entrusted the chieftaincy – *ceann-cinnidh* – to his kinsman Roland.

The new clan chief could not live at Turnberry, of course. That privilege was reserved for Countess Marjorie, Neil's daughter, whose marriage to Bruce of Annandale removed the castle from the Kennedy hegemony. But Roland and his heirs lived not far away, at Dunure up the coast.

Judging from the prefix *dun-*, the site probably originated in the first millennium AD, though we do not know when the Kennedys acquired it. Roland probably, and his son John certainly, were lords of the castle. Time and tide have not been kind to this once-formidable fortress.

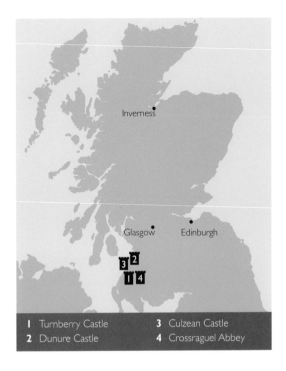

| 1 Turnberry Castle | 3 Culzean Castle |
| 2 Dunure Castle | 4 Crossraguel Abbey |

The lofty stone pinnacle at the cliff edge is a remnant of the original 13th-century tower of the clan chief, while later buildings cascade down from the rocky knoll and over the original rock-cut ditch. It is difficult to imagine Mary Queen of Scots enjoying her stay here in 1563 – even though it was at the height of summer.

The armed assault on Dunure, following the roasting of the hapless Abbot of Crossraguel therein in 1569, is said to have caused considerable structural damage, and it may have been shortly thereafter that the Kennedy chiefs relocated to another Ayrshire cliff edge, overlooking Culzean Bay. Derived from the Gaelic *cuil eun* – meaning 'bird's neuk' – Culzean is an apt description of this rocky perch. Traces of a 16th-century tower survive, entombed in the present handsome edifice, built for the earls of Cassillis in the late 18th century. Culzean was a castle only in name; in reality it was a magnificent castellated country seat worthy of the Age of Enlightenment in which it was built.

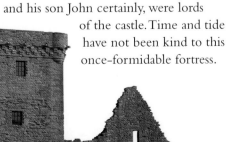

CLAN
DONALD

This page: Castle Tioram, on an island in Loch Moidart, became the seat of the MacDonalds of Clanranald in the 14th century.

'One effort more, and Scotland's free!
Lord of the Isles, my trust in thee
Is firm as Ailsa-rock.'

Sir Walter Scott

Left: Heather, the plant badge of the MacDonalds.

Below: The MacDonald crest badge. The Latin motto translates as, 'By sea, by land'.

THE STORY OF CLAN DONALD

Two great clans rose to pre-eminence during the 14th century to take centre stage in Scottish politics – the Stewarts and the MacDonalds. They couldn't have been more different. The Stewarts were Lowlanders, with ancestral roots reaching back to Norman France. The MacDonalds, on the other hand, were indigenous to the Hebrides, with origins firmly rooted in the Gaelic–Norse empire that emerged following the Viking incursions in the 9th century. While the Stewarts represented the new feudal order, the MacDonalds remained thoroughly Celtic.

The two great aristocratic houses had one thing in common, however. Both had royal aspirations. So when the Stewarts ascended the throne of Scotland in 1371, the MacDonald Lords of the Isles, with the blood of Somerled coursing through their veins, saw an opportunity to advance their own position. The stage was set for an epic battle of wills. The century-long struggle between the Stewarts and MacDonalds was not just a clash of two clans, it was a clash of two cultures, whose outcome would effectively determine what kind of country Scotland became. That struggle, and its outcome, still resonates to this day.

The Donald from whom the clan derives its name was the grandson of the great Somerled. In the early 12th century, Somerled, *Rí Airir Goidel* ('King of Argyll'), emerged as one of two mighty warlords in the Hebrides. In 1158, he finally defeated his brother-in-law, Godfrey, King of Man, in a great sea battle, and became

also *Rí Innse Gall* ('King of the Isles of the Foreigners'). He now ruled over all the islands from Man to Lewis. But still he wasn't satisfied. In 1164, he sailed his huge fleet eastward into the Firth of Clyde, heading for the very heart of the Scottish kingdom. It proved his undoing. He was killed near Renfrew Castle, seat of the Steward of Scotland; his severed head was borne to Glasgow Cathedral as a war trophy.

Somerled's demise saw his vast empire fragment, his sons dividing up his inheritance, as was the Gaelic custom. Dugald, probably the eldest, became *Rí Airir Goidel*, ruling over Argyll and the southern isles; he founded Clan MacDougall. Ranald, the second son, assumed the title *Rí Innse Gall*, ruling over Kintyre and Islay. Ranald's two sons, Ruari and Donald, each formed an important clan. The MacRuaris have lapsed in prominence, but you'd be hard-pressed to find a telephone book anywhere in the world without a MacDonald in it.

We know next to nothing about Donald, other than that he led his clansmen into battles from Ulster to Moray. Clan Donald would in time become foremost among the descendants of Somerled, but in Donald's day they were less significant than the MacDougalls. Then came the Wars

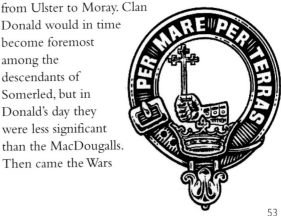

of Independence with England, when noble families across Scotland had to declare their loyalties. The MacDougalls sided with King John Balliol, Edward I's 'puppet'. Donald's son and grandson, Angus Mór and Angus Óg, threw in their lot with King Robert Bruce. And when 'wee Angus' and his 5,000 Islesmen helped Bruce to victory at Bannockburn in 1314, the destiny of Somerled's descendants was settled. The MacDougalls were forfeited and their lands, including Jura, Coll, Tiree, Glencoe, Morvern and Lochaber, granted to the MacDonalds. Angus died in 1330, and had chosen not to be buried at Saddell Abbey, in Kintyre, but on Iona, inauguration place of the ancient kings of Dál Riata. The dying embers of the old Kingship of the Isles were being fanned into life once more.

Thereafter, Clan Donald's rise was meteoric. By 1336, Angus's son, John, was styling himself 'Lord of the Isles'. Marriage to his cousin Amy, heiress of the MacRuari dominions, brought him Knoydart, Moidart, Mull, Rum, the Uists and Barra. And in 1343, David II, Bruce's son, granted him Lewis and Harris as well. It was as if Lord John was reassembling Somerled's lost kingdom.

But John also recognised that the political landscape had changed out of all recognition since Somerled's day. Where once two crowns – Norway and Scotland – had fought over the Hebrides, now just the kings of Scots remained. John had no recourse other than to ingratiate himself with them. So he began climbing the greasy Scottish pole. In 1350 he divorced Amy and married Lady Margaret, daughter of Robert the Steward. And in 1371, when the Steward became Robert II, John found himself part of the royal establishment, the king's brother-in-law and one of the most powerful men in the realm. By the time of his death at Ardtornish Castle in 1387, he was ruling over a vast Hebridean empire, in which branches of MacDonalds had opened up all over the place; they even had one in Ulster.

But John's son, Donald, wasn't content with just the Hebrides: he wanted more. In 1402, the death of his brother-in-law the Earl of Ross, without male issue, provided a golden opportunity. Donald stormed up the Great Glen to secure the earldom by force. The great castles of Urquhart, Inverness and Dingwall fell into his lap. So too did the Isle of Skye, part of the Ross hegemony. The MacLeods,

Right: Albrecht Dürer's painting of gallowglasses (literally 'foreign soldiers'). Though associated with Ireland, these highly effective medieval mercenaries were largely recruited from the MacDonald clan.

Far left: Urquhart Castle on Loch Ness, not far from Inverness. Throughout the 15th century, this royal stronghold was repeatedly raided and captured by marauding MacDonalds.

Left: The grave slab of Gilbride, chief of the MacKinnons and a member of Clan Donald's ruling 'Council of the Isles'.

hitherto the main clan on the island, were far from happy. The story goes that a MacDonald clansman was out inspecting his new property when he slipped on a cliff edge and was only prevented from falling to his death when he grabbed at a sod of grass. A MacLeod woman, hearing his cries for help, came over and muttered: 'Ah well, ye've taken everything else, so ye may as well tak this as well.' With that she gave the sod a kick, sending the poor MacDonald to his death.

Despite these new acquisitions, the newly-ennobled Earl of Ross was not satisfied. While the Stewart court was indulging in an internal power struggle, Donald marched out from the Highlands in 1411 at the head of a 10,000-strong army, comprising not just MacDonalds but also Camerons, MacKinnons, MacKintoshes, MacLeans and MacLeods. Only a hastily assembled army of Lowland clans stood in his way. The two armies met at Harlaw, near Inverurie. That bloody but indecisive battle was a landmark in Scottish history, for it was the first fought between Highlander and Lowlander. The last, three centuries later at Culloden, would also involve the MacDonalds.

' Oh, cam ye frae the Hielans, man?
And cam ye a' the wye?
Saw ye MacDonal and his men
Come marching frae the Skye?'

From a traditional Aberdeenshire ballad

Donald 'of Harlaw' claimed the victory but the Stewarts were alert to the power of rumour. They spread tales of strangely attired 'wyld wykkyd Helandmen' descending from their mountain fastnesses on poor, civilised Lowlanders. King and Lord now shared a mutual mistrust. For the remainder of the century, the two played out a deadly game of cat and mouse, on which the sovereign future of Scotland depended.

DID YOU KNOW...

At the Battle of Bannockburn in 1314, Angus Óg MacDonald and his Islesmen led the right flank for King Robert Bruce, a position subsequent MacDonald chiefs regarded as their right. But at Culloden in 1746 Prince Charles Edward Stuart denied them that privilege, positioning them on the left. Was this slight to their honour perhaps the reason for their belated rush into the action on that fateful day?

In 1462, unknown to all but a privileged few, John, 4th Lord of the Isles, entered into a secret pact with Edward IV of England and the recently disgraced 9th Earl of Douglas. Under the so-called Treaty of Westminster–Ardtornish, all three were to work together to destroy the Stewart dynasty and carve up Scotland. England would get southern Scotland, leaving the MacDonalds and Douglases to fight over the rest. When word of the pact eventually reached the ears of the Royal Stewarts, it spelled the end of the Lordship of the Isles. Lord John was finally stripped of all his lands and titles in 1493, and died in 1503, not at mighty Ardtornish but in a modest Dundee lodging house. The Lordship of the Isles died with him; Somerled's dynasty was no more. After four centuries of political and military manoeuvrings, feudal Scotland had finally prevailed over its ancient Celtic past.

'It is no joy without Clan Donald,
It is no strength to be without them;
The best race in the round world.'

Giolla Coluim mac an Ollaimh, 15th century

Clan Donald did its utmost to recover the situation, and no less than seven attempts were made over the next 50 years. In 1539, for example, Donald Gorm MacDonald of Sleat rose up, only to be killed by an arrow in the eye, fired from the battlements of Eilean Donan Castle. That insurrection brought James V in person to the Hebrides, and his visit lives on in the Isle of Skye: the place-name Portree is from the Gaelic *port righ*, meaning 'king's harbour'.

The last throw of the dice came in 1545 when Donald Dubh – 'Black Donald', Lord John's grandson – amassed a fleet of 180 galleys and 4,000 men in Ireland. Alas, he caught a fever in Drogheda and died. The planned uprising petered out.

The downfall of the Lordship of the Isles spelled political and cultural disaster, not only for the MacDonalds but for all Gaels. No more would individual clans, such as the MacLeans, Macleods and Macneils, be united under one overlord, governing the Hebrides as the Council of the Isles. Henceforth, each would look to its own, with inevitable consequences.

Left: Eilean Donan Castle, on an island in Loch Duich in the western Highlands. This was the scene of Donald Gorm MacDonald's final, desperate struggle to recover the Lordship of the Isles in 1539.

DID YOU KNOW...

The first recorded incident in the long and bitter feud between the MacDonalds and the Campbells was in 1427 when John Mór MacDonald, founder of the MacDonalds of Dunyvaig and the Glens, was murdered by John MacArthur, a Campbell, at Ard Dubh, on Islay. The assassination was allegedly carried out at the behest of James I. It was not the last murderous deed the Campbells would commit against the MacDonalds at royal command.

Feuding became a way of life, and the post-Lordship age became *linn nan creach* 'the age of the raid', in which the MacDonald cadets – Ardnamurchan, Clanranald, Dunyvaig and the Glens, Glencoe, Glengarry, Keppoch and Sleat – played their part. Into the power vacuum stepped outsiders, most notably the Campbells of Argyll, lording it over the Gaels with an iron fist. At the infamous Massacre of Glencoe of 1692, soldiers from Argyll's Regiment murdered MacIain of Glencoe and most of his household one cold February morning. But this was just one of many atrocities perpetrated by all sides.

The MacDonalds and the other clans would come together again. Following the overthrow of James VII & II by William and Mary in 1689, they formed the backbone of the Jacobite army that fought so valiantly at Killiecrankie (1689), at Sheriffmuir (1715), at Glenshiel (1719) and most memorably of all at Culloden (1746). They fought to restore to the throne those they felt to be the lawful dynasty, the Stewarts. What irony, for it had been the Stewarts who had brought about their downfall.

THE MACDONALDS

1158	**Somerled 'King of Argyll'** establishes himself as 'King of the Isles'.
1164	**Somerled** killed at Renfrew while invading Scotland. Succeeded by three sons. The second, **Ranald**, takes title 'King of the Isles', ruling from Islay.
c.1200	**Ranald** founds Iona Abbey and Nunnery.
1207	**Ranald** succeeded by son Donald, founder of Clan Donald.
c.1250	**Donald** succeeded by son Angus Mór ('Big Angus').
1300	**Angus Mór** succeeded by his son, **Angus Óg**. Angus Mór's younger sons found Maclains of Glencoe and Maclains of Ardnamurchan.
1314	**Angus Óg** brings 5,000 men to fight for King Robert Bruce at Bannockburn.
1330	**Angus Óg** succeeded by his son John.
1337	**John** marries cousin **Amy**, heiress of Clan MacRuari, and acquires Knoydart, Moidart, Rum, the Uists and Barra. First to be styled 'Lord of the Isles'. Their eldest son founds MacDonalds of Clanranald.
1343	**John** acquires Lewis and Harris.
1350	**John** divorces Amy and marries **Margaret**, daughter of Robert the Steward (future Robert II). Their sons found MacDonalds of Dunyvaig and the Glens, Glengarry, and Keppoch.
1360	**John** appointed keeper of Edinburgh Castle by David II.
1387	**John** dies at Ardtornish Castle. Succeeded by son **Donald 'of Harlaw'**.
1411	**Donald** fights inconclusive Battle of Harlaw against royal army. Secures Earldom of Ross, including Isle of Skye.
1423	**Donald** dies at Ardtornish, one of the most powerful men in Scotland. Succeeded by son **Alexander**.
1427	Donald's brother, **John Mór Tanister**, murdered on Islay by a Campbell. First recorded incident in the notorious MacDonald – Campbell feud.
1429	**Alexander** captured in Lochaber and imprisoned in Tantallon Castle.
1431	**MacDonalds** rout royal army at Inverlochy. Alexander reinstated as Lord of the Isles and Earl of Ross.
1449	**Alexander dies** at Dingwall Castle. Succeeded by son John.
1462	**John** signs secret pact with Edward IV of England and exiled Earl of Douglas to divide Scotland between them.

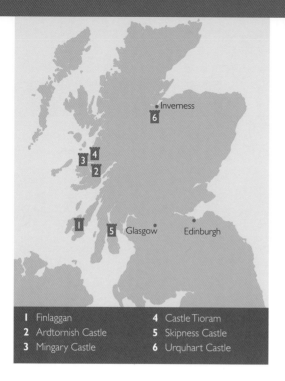

1 Finlaggan	**4** Castle Tioram
2 Ardtornish Castle	**5** Skipness Castle
3 Mingary Castle	**6** Urquhart Castle

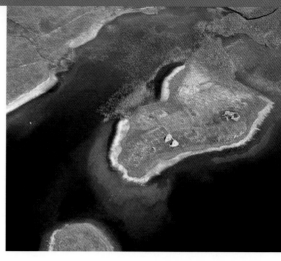

Above: Finlaggan on the Isle of Islay, spiritual home of Clan Donald, where the Council of the Isles met.

Opposite: Ardtornish Castle, overlooking the Sound of Mull, where two Lords of the Isles died.

CASTLES OF THE MACDONALDS

The MacDonald Lords of the Isles were among the most powerful men in Scotland throughout the late Middle Ages, the great age of castle-building – and yet they themselves built no great castles. The other sons of Somerled did. The MacDougalls built mighty Dunstaffnage, near Oban, and the MacRuaris the equally-forbidding Castle Tioram on Loch Moidart.

It is true that the MacDonalds acquired a number of great castles down the years as their tentacles spread across the Hebrides and beyond, among them Skipness, Urquhart and Dunluce, in Ulster. But they weren't the builders. The castles they erected at their own hand were modest by the standards set by their peers. It was as if they were so strong, so confident of their place at the apex of Gaelic society, that they had no need for grim defences.

Their chief seat on Islay perfectly embodied this, for it was no forbidding stronghold perched atop a sea-girt rock, but a cluster of buildings on two low-lying islands in an inland loch. Finlaggan is more a work of nature than of man – Eilean Mór ('the Big Isle') and the smaller Eilean na Comhairle ('the Council Isle'). These two islets lay at the heart of the MacDonald empire for over 400 years. It was here that most of their chiefs were inaugurated, in an elaborate ritual that centred on the act of the new chief placing his foot into a footprint carved out of solid rock, denoting that he should walk in the footsteps and uprightness of his forebears. When the ceremony was over, the feasting continued for over a week.

Finlaggan was also where the Council of the Isles gathered to discuss its business. The equivalent of a Privy Council, it included not just MacDonald chieftains but also other clan chiefs who acknowledged the overlordship of the Lords of the Isles. These included MacLean of Duart, MacLeod of Dunvegan and Harris, and Macneil of Barra. They conducted their business on Eilean na Comhairle, and resided on Eilean Mór. The administration they presided over was highly bureaucratic. There were bards (the MacVurichs) and physicians (the MacBeths –

'sons of life'), travel agents (the MacEachrans), filing clerks (the MacDuffies) and a weights and measures department (the MacKinnons). Equally important, given the politics of the day, were the council's spin doctors, the MacLaverties.

Finlaggan was probably reserved for formal occasions such as inaugurations and gatherings of the council, the chiefs of Clan Donald normally residing elsewhere. Their main residence on Islay may well have been Dunyvaig Castle, on the south coast. Its place-name, 'fort of the bay', suggests a history reaching back to the coming of the Gaels to the Hebrides from Ireland in Roman times.

Their chief seat in Kintyre was almost certainly Dunaverty Castle, south of Campbeltown, where Angus Óg sheltered Robert Bruce in 1306 after the defeat at Methven. Dunaverty achieved royal notoriety of a different sort in 1493, when John MacDonald, of Dunyvaig and the Glens, recaptured his castle from James IV after the forfeiture of the Lords of the Isles. He then proceeded to hang its newly-installed royal keeper from the battlements – in full view of the departing sovereign.

The prodigious expansion of the MacDonald empire during the 14th century saw the epicentre shift northward, leaving Islay and Kintyre on the periphery. While Finlaggan retained its ceremonial and courtly functions, for practical reasons the Lords of the Isles relocated north also, to Ardtornish Castle, in Morvern. The 1st and 2nd Lords of the Isles

THE MACDONALDS CONT.

1476	**John** stripped of Earldom of Ross by James III, but allowed to retain title 'Lord of the Isles'. Son **Angus Óg** breaks with father to regain forfeited Earldom.
1481	**Angus Óg** defeats John at 'Battle of the Bloody Bay', becoming effective chief of Clan Donald.
1490	**Angus Óg** murdered in Inverness Castle.
1493	**John** forfeited again. James IV receives submission of **MacDonald cadets** at Dunstaffnage Castle.
1500	**James IV** appoints **Archibald Campbell**, Earl of Argyll, Lieutenant-General in the Isles, to snuff out MacDonald unrest.
1501	Angus Óg's son, **Donald Dubh**, escapes from Innis Chonnell Castle.
1503	**John**, last Lord of the Isles, dies in Dundee.
1506	**Donald Dubh** recaptured and imprisoned in Stirling Castle.
1543	**Donald Dubh** escapes from Edinburgh Castle, and proclaims himself Lord of the Isles.
1545	**Donald Dubh** seals pact with Henry VIII of England but dies in Ireland, preparing to invade Scotland. Last attempt to restore Lordship of the Isles.
1612	**Angus** MacDonald of Dunyvaig and the Glens sells Islay, ancient heartland of the MacDonalds.
1689	**MacDonalds** help defeat King William's army at Killiecrankie.
1692	**MacDonalds** murdered by soldiers from Argyll's Regiment in infamous Massacre of Glencoe.
1746	**MacDonalds** lead the Jacobite left flank at Culloden.

This picture: Mingary Castle in Ardnamurchan, in the western Highlands, which withstood bombardment by a vessel of the Spanish Armada in 1588.

Above: Skipness Castle, in Knapdale, Argyll. Built by the MacSweens, it was one of several castles acquired by the warlike MacDonalds.

died there. For a while in the 15th century their descendants resided also at Dingwall Castle, in their capacity as Earls of Ross; the 3rd Lord died there in 1449.

Dingwall Castle has largely gone, but Ardtornish remains. Here, too, the castle is not what we might expect of a great lord. Its two-storey hall-house is not hidden behind a massive wall; instead it stands exposed, surrounded by a complex of ruined structures and courts, reminiscent of Finlaggan.

Such was the all-pervading power of Clan Donald that there is hardly a castle in the Hebrides not linked to them. They either built them or else acquired them through marriage, by grant or via more nefarious means. They ruled from them and died in them. They even incarcerated their own kinsmen in them, as the unfortunate Uisdean MacGilleasbuig Chleirich found to his cost in 1602. Uisdean – or Hugh – was a notorious pirate who had designs on becoming chief of the MacDonalds of Sleat. He hatched a plan to kill Donald Gorm Mór of Sleat and other leading clansmen during a housewarming gathering to celebrate the completion of his new Skye residence, Caisteal Uisdean ('Hugh's Castle').

The plot was foiled when letters of invitation were delivered to the wrong people. One was addressed to an accomplice; the other to the chief himself. Hugh was chased to Dun an Sticir, on North Uist, and eventually caught there, disguised as an old crone. He was taken to Duntulm, the chief's own residence back on Skye. There he was thrown into the dungeon, and fed on a diet of salted beef and no water. We don't know how long Hugh took to die, but his ghostly groans are said to haunt the ruins of Duntulm still.

Many another castle not owned by Clan Donald was attacked by them at some time or another, but none more so than mighty Urquhart Castle, beside Loch Ness. Countless times after 1395, the MacDonalds swept up the Great Glen and past Urquhart, then a royal

DID YOU KNOW...

The 3rd Lord of the Isles spent over two years in prison. In June 1429 he was captured in Lochaber during a skirmish with a force headed by James I. The king had him taken to Edinburgh, where he was humiliated in front of his peers at the high altar of Holyrood Abbey before being hauled off to mighty Tantallon Castle. And there he languished until Queen Joan interceded on his behalf and secured his release, late in 1431.

Above: Dun an Sticir, on North Uist, where the pirate Hugh MacDonald was eventually captured.

Below: An artist's impression of the Great Raid of 1545, in which MacDonald raiders wrought devastation at Urquhart Castle.

stronghold, en route to Inverness in pursuit of their goal to become Earls of Ross. For 150 years, the castle passed back and forth between the Royal Stewarts and the Lords of the Isles like a bone between two dogs.

In despair, the Crown handed responsibility for the stronghold to loyal supporters, first the Gordons, then the Grants. But they fared no better – until 1545, when the MacDonalds rampaged through the glen one last time. They took away 3,000 sheep, 2,000 cattle, 2,000 goats, 383 horses, 122 swine, 64 geese – and from the castle itself 12 feather beds and other furniture, brewing vats and roasting spits, a chest containing £300, gunpowder, stands of armour and three boats. Not for nothing was this incident called the Great Raid.

The castles of Clan Donald are not only among the oldest in Scotland, they are also among the last to figure in warfare, proving their worth right up to Culloden and beyond. Mingary, in Ardnamurchan, is a good example. In 1588, following the scattering of the Spanish Armada, it withstood bombardment from a Spanish galleon, the *Florida*, that had taken shelter in Tobermory Bay and been purloined by Lachlan MacLean of Duart,

then in feud with the MacDonalds. During the Civil War of the 1640s its garrison beat off another assault; though this time the MacDonalds themselves did the attacking, the stronghold having fallen into the hands of their deadliest enemies, the Campbells.

A century later Mingary was still being garrisoned, this time by government redcoats outstationed from Fort William. Prince Charles Edward Stuart had first set foot on the British mainland in the summer of 1745, not far from the castle, and the Campbells were quick to dispatch a force to patrol the area. Despite the passage of 500 years, Mingary was still fit for purpose.

Bonnie Prince Charlie contrived to negotiate his way past Mingary and Fort William, and almost succeeded in restoring the Stewarts to the throne of Great Britain. But his dream was trampled into the mud of Culloden on 16 April 1746, along with any hopes Clan Donald had of returning to their rightful place as Lords of the Isles.

CASTLE LOCATION DIRECTORY

Road directions, Ordnance Survey map references and telephone numbers (where appropriate) are given below for each building mentioned in this book.

PLEASE NOTE:
Private properties are not normally open to the public.

Visitors are usually welcomed at properties in the care of Historic Scotland, the National Trust for Scotland and local authorities. Some properties owned by members of the Historic Houses Association are also open to the public.

Many of these properties operate seasonal opening hours and may be closed during the winter months. Readers are advised to telephone before visiting.

Aberdour Castle (HS)
In Aberdour, Fife, 5 miles (8km) east of the Forth Bridges on the A921.
OS: NT 192 854
Tel: 01383 860 519

Ardtornish Estate (Private)
In Morvern, near Oban, Argyll & Bute, reached via the Corran Ferry, 8 miles (13km) SW of Fort William on the A82.
OS: NM 702 475

Argyll's Lodging (HS)
Just below the castle in Stirling, off the M9.
OS: NS 792 938
Tel: 01786 431 319

Auchindoun Castle (HS)
Two miles (3km) south of Dufftown, Moray, on the A941.
OS: NJ 349 374
Tel: 01667 460 232

Balvenie Castle (HS)
At Dufftown, Moray, on the A94.
OS: NJ 326 408
Tel: 01340 820 121

Berwick Castle (EH)
In the centre of Berwick-upon-Tweed, Northumbria, on the A1.
OS: NT 993 534
Tel: 0870 333 1181

Blair Castle (HHA)
At Blair Atholl, near Pitlochry, Perth & Kinross, on the A9.
OS: NN 864 660
Tel: 01796 481 207

Bog o' Gight also called **Gight Castle** (Private)
Three miles (5km) east of Fyvie, Aberdeenshire, off the B9005.
OS: NJ 827 392

Bothwell Castle (HS)
In Uddingston, South Lanarkshire, off the B707.
OS: NS 688 593
Tel: 01698 816 894

Brodick Castle (NTS)
On the Isle of Arran, 1.5 miles (2.5km) north of Brodick town centre.
OS: NS 015 378
Tel: 08444 932 152

Cairnbulg Castle (Private)
Two miles (3km) SE of Fraserburgh, Aberdeenshire, off the B9033.
OS: NK 015 639

Castle Campbell (HS)
At the head of Dollar Glen, Dollar, Clackmannanshire, 10 miles (16km) east of Stirling on the A91.
OS: NS 961 993
Tel: 01259 742 408

Carlisle Castle (EH)
In the centre of Carlisle, Cumbria, off the M6.
OS: NY 397 563
Tel: 01228 591 922

Carnasserie Castle (HS)
Two miles (3km) north of Kilmartin, Argyll & Bute, off the A816.
OS: NM 839 009
Tel: 0131 668 8800

Cawdor Castle (HHA)
Between Inverness and Nairn, Highland, on the B9090 off the A96.
OS: NH 847 498
Tel: 01667 404 401

Corgarff Castle (HS)
Eight miles (13km) west of Strathdon, Aberdeenshire, on the A939.
OS: NJ 254 086
Tel: 01975 651460

Crichton Castle (HS)
Two and a half miles (4km) SW of Pathhead, Midlothian, off the A68.
OS: NT 380 611
Tel: 01875 320 017

Crookston Castle (HS)
Off Brockburn Road, Pollok, SW of Glasgow city centre. Exit M8 at Junction 26.
OS: NS 525 627
Tel: 0141 883 9606

Crossraguel Abbey (HS)
Two miles (3km) south of Maybole, South Ayrshire, on the A77.
OS: NS 275 083
Tel: 01655 883113

Culzean Castle (NTS)
Twelve miles (19km) south of Ayr, South Ayrshire on the A719.
OS: NS 232 103
Tel: 08444 932 149

Doune Castle (HS)
In Doune, Stirlingshire, 10 miles (16km) NW of Stirling off the A84.
OS: NN 725 014
Tel: 01786 841 742

Drumlanrig Castle (HHA)
Near Carronbridge, 17 miles (27km) NW of Dumfries, Dumfries & Galloway, off the A76.
OS: NX 851 992
Tel: 01848 331 555

Dumbarton Castle (HS)
In Dumbarton, West Dunbartonshire, on the A82.
OS: NS 398 744
Tel: 01389 732 167

Dun an Sticir (Private)
Near Newtonferry on the island of North Uist.
OS: NF 897 776

Dundonald Castle (HS)
In the centre of Dundonald village, 5 miles (8km) east of Troon, South Ayrshire.
OS: NS 364 345
Tel: 01563 851 489

Dunfermline Palace (HS)
In Dunfermline, Fife, off the M90.
OS: NT 090 873
Tel: 01383 739 026

Dunstaffnage Castle (HS)
Near Dunbeg, 3 miles (5km) north of Oban, Argyll & Bute, off the A85.
OS: NM 882 344
Tel: 01631 562 465

Dunure Castle (LA)
In the village of Dunure, 6 miles (10km) SW of Ayr, South Ayrshire, on the A719.
OS: NS 252 158

Dunyvaig Castle (Private)
On the Isle of Islay, near Lagavulin Distillery, 3 miles (5km) east of Port Ellen on the A846.
OS: NR 405 454

The Earl's Palace, Birsay (HS)
On the NW tip of the Orkney mainland, 25 miles (40km) NW of Kirkwall on the A966.
OS: HY 248 277
Tel: 01856 721 205

The Earl's Palace, Kirkwall (HS)
Next to St Magnus Cathedral in the centre of Kirkwall, Orkney, on the A960.
OS: HY 448 108
Tel: 01856 721 205

Edinburgh Castle (HS)
In central Edinburgh, at the top of the Royal Mile.
OS: NT 251 735
Tel: 0131 225 9846

Eilean Donan Castle (Private)
On an island
south of Dornie,
Highland,
off the A87.
OS: NG 881 259
Tel: 01599 555 202

Elgin Castle (LA)
In Elgin, Moray,
on the A96.
OS: NJ 211 628

Elgin Cathedral (HS)
In Elgin, Moray,
on the A96.
OS: NJ 221 630
Tel: 01343 547 171

Falkland Palace (NTS)
In the village of
Falkland, Fife,
11 miles (17.5km)
north of Kirkcaldy
on the A912.
OS: NO 253 075
Tel: 08444 932 186

Finlaggan
(Private)
On the Isle of Islay,
2 miles (3km) NW
of Ballygrant,
off the A846.
OS: NR 388 681

Castle Fraser (NTS)
Four miles (6.5km)
north of Dunecht,
Aberdeenshire,
off the A944.
OS: NJ 722 125
Tel: 08444 932 164

Glenbuchat Castle (HS)
Ten miles (16km)
west of Alford,
Aberdeenshire,
on the A97.
OS: NJ 397 149
Tel: 01667 460 232

Greenknowe Tower (HS)
Six miles (10km)
east of Lauder,
Scottish Borders,
on the A6105.
OS: NT 639 428
Tel: 0131 668 8800

Hermitage Castle (HS)
Five miles (8km)
NE of Newcastleton,
Scottish Borders,
on the B6399.
OS: NY 497 961
Tel: 01387 376 222

The Palace of Holyroodhouse
(Royal residence)
In central Edinburgh,
at the foot of the
Royal Mile.
OS: NT 268 739
Tel: 0131 556 5100

Huntly Castle (HS)
In Huntly, Aberdeenshire,
on the A96.
OS: NJ 532 407
Tel: 01466 793191

Iona Abbey & Nunnery (HS)
On the island of Iona,
reached via ferry
from Fionnphort
on the Isle of Mull.
OS: NM 286 245
Tel: 01681 700 512

Innis Chonnell
(Private)
On an islet off the SE
shore of Loch Awe, 25
miles (40km) SW of
Dalmally, Argyll & Bute,
on the B840.
OS: NM 976 119

Inveraray Castle (HHA)
In Inveraray, Argyll &
Bute, near the NW tip
of Loch Fyne, on the A83.
OS: NN 093 092
Tel: 01499 302 203

Inverness Castle (LA)
In Inverness city centre.
OS: NH 667 451

Jarlshof (HS)
At the southern tip
of the Shetland mainland,
half a mile (1km) from
Sumburgh airport; 22
miles (35km) south of
Lerwick on the A970.
OS: HU 396 096
Tel: 01950 460 112

Castle Kennedy (Private)
Five miles (8km)
east of Stranraer,
Dumfries & Galloway,
on the A75.
OS: NX 114 608
Tel: 01581 400 225

Kilchurn Castle (HS)
At the NE tip of Loch
Awe, 2.5 miles (4km)
west of Dalmally, Argyll &
Bute, off the A85. Public
access on foot or by boat.
OS: NN 133 276
Tel: 0131 668 8800

Kinnaird Head Lighthouse (HS)
On a promontory
just north of
Fraserburgh,
Aberdeenshire,
on the A92.
OS: NJ 999 677
Tel: 01346 511 022

Linlithgow Palace (HS)
In the centre of
Linlithgow, West
Lothian, off the M9.
OS: NT 001 772
Tel: 01506 842 896

Loch an Eilean
(Private)
Four miles (6.5km)
south of Aviemore,
Highland, off the B970.
OS: NH 898 079

Lochleven Castle (HS)
On an island in
Loch Leven reached by
boat from Kinross, Perth
& Kinross, off the M90.
OS: NO 137 017
Tel: 07778 040 483

Lochmaben Castle (HS)
On Lochmaben Castle
Loch, 3 miles (5km) west
of Lockerbie, Dumfries &
Galloway, on the A709.
OS: NY 088 811
Tel: 0131 668 8800

Menstrie Castle (NTS)
Five miles (8km) NE
of Stirling, in Menstrie,
Clackmannanshire,
off the A91.
OS: NS 850 967
Tel: 01259 212478

Mingary Castle
(Private)
One mile (1.5km) SE of
Kilchoan, Arnamurchan,
Highland, off the B8007.
OS: NM 502 631

Morton Castle (HS)
Two miles (3km) NE of
Carronbridge, Dumfries
& Galloway, off the A702.
OS: NX 890 992
Tel: 0131 668 8800

Newark Castle (HS)
In Port Glasgow,
Inverclyde, 12 miles
(20km) NW of Paisley on
the A8.
OS: NS 328 745
Tel: 01475 741 858

Caisteal na Nighinn Ruaidhe (Private)
On Loch Avich, Argyll
& Bute, 20 miles (32km)
SE of Oban off the A816.
OS: NM 9166 1375

Rothesay Castle (HS)
In Rothesay on the
Isle of Bute. Ferry from
Wemyss Bay, Inverclyde,
on the A78.
OS: NS 088 645
Tel: 01700 502 691

Roxburgh Castle (Private)
One mile (1.5km)
SW of Kelso, Scottish
Borders, on the A699.
OS: NT 712 337

Ruthven Barracks (HS)
One mile (1.5km)
south of Kingussie,
Highland, signposted
from the A9
and the A86.
OS: NN 764 997
Tel: 01667 460 232

St Bride's Church, Douglas (HS)
In Douglas, South
Lanarkshire,
10 miles (16km)
SW of Lanark,
off the A70.
OS: NS 835 309
Tel: 01555 851 657

Scalloway Castle (HS)
In Scalloway, 6 miles
(10km) SW of
Lerwick, Shetland,
on the A970. Collect
key from local hotel.
OS: HU 404 392
Tel: 01667 460 232

Skipness Castle (HS)
Fifteen miles (24km)
by road south of
Tarbert, Argyll & Bute,
on the east coast of
Kintyre, off the B8001.
OS: NR 907 577
Tel: 0131 668 8800

Castle Stalker
(Private)
On an island in Loch
Laich accessible by boat
from Portnacroish,
23 miles (37km)
north of Oban,
Argyll & Bute.
OS: NM 921 473
Tel: 01631 740 315

Castle Sween (HS)
On the east shore
of Loch Sween,
in Knapdale,
Argyll & Bute,
off the B8025.
OS: NR 712 788
Tel: 0131 668 8800

Stirling Castle (HS)
At the top of the
old town of Stirling,
off the M9.
OS: NS 788 941
Tel: 01786 450 000

Tantallon Castle (HS)
Three miles (5km)
east of North
Berwick, East Lothian,
off the A198.
OS: NT 595 850
Tel: 01620 892 727

Threave Castle (HS)
On an island three
miles (5km) west
of Castle Douglas,
Dumfries & Galloway,
on the A75.
OS: NX 739 623
Tel: 07711 223 101

Castle Tioram
(Private)
On a rocky
island in
Loch Moidart,
Highland, off the
A861. Accessible
only at low tide.
OS: NM 662 723

Traquair House (HHA)
One and half miles
(2.5km) south
of Innerleithen,
Scottish Borders
on the B709.
OS: NT 330 354
Tel: 01896 830 323

Turnberry Castle (Private)
Next to Turnberry
golf course,
six miles (10km) SW
of Maybole,
South Ayrshire,
off the A719.
OS: NS 196 072

Urquhart Castle (HS)
On Loch Ness near
Drumnadrochit,
Highland, on the A82.
OS: NH 531 286
Tel: 01456 450 551

EXPLORER PASS

For visitors to Scotland, the Explorer Pass offers admission to all Historic Scotland properties for 3 or 7 days. Ask for details and prices at any Historic Scotland property or visit our website at www.historic-scotland.gov.uk/explorer

HISTORIC SCOTLAND MEMBERSHIP

Historic Scotland Membership offers fantastic days out all year, plus many other benefits, discounts and special offers. Membership is available for 12 months or for life, in a variety of different categories.

HISTORIC SCOTLAND MEMBERSHIP

Entry to over 300 Historic Scotland sites as often as you want

- Quarterly membership magazine
- Member discount in Historic Scotland's shops, both online and at individual sites
- Access to over 500 historic sites in the care of English Heritage, Cadw (Wales) and Manx National Heritage (Isle of Man)

HOW TO JOIN

There are four ways you can obtain more information or start your membership:

In person: At any staffed Historic Scotland site or property

By phone: Call [+44] (0)131 668 8999 with your credit/debit card details

On-line: www.historic-scotland.gov.uk/member

By post to: Membership of Historic Scotland, Longmore House, Salisbury Place Edinburgh EH9 1SH.

FURTHER READING AND CREDITS

P. Anderson *Black Patie: The Life and Times of Patrick, Earl of Orkney, Lord of Shetland* (1992)

J. Balfour Paul *The Scots Peerage* (1904–07)

G. W. S. Barrow *The Kingdom of the Scots* (1973)

S. Boardman *The Campbells 1250–1513* (2006)

M. Brown *The Black Douglases: War and Lordship in Late Medieval Scotland 1300–1455* (1998)

A. Campbell of Airds *A History of Clan Campbell*, 3 vols (2000–04)

J. Dunbar *Scottish Royal Palaces* (1999)

C. I. Fraser *The Clan Fraser of Lovat* (1979)

Flora M. Fraser *Clan Fraser* (1997)

J. Fraser *Chronicles of the Fraser* (1905)

W. Fraser *The Red Book of Menteith* (1880)

W. Fraser *The Douglas Book* 3 vols (1885)

A. & A. Macdonald *The Clan Donald* 3 vols (1896–1904)

D. J. Macdonald of Castleton *Clan Donald* (1978)

C. McKean *The Scottish Château* (2001)

H. L. MacQueen 'The Kin of Kennedy, "Kenkynnol" and the Common Law', in A. Grant & K. J. Stringer (eds) *Medieval Scotland: Crown, Lordship and Community* (1993)

H. L. MacQueen 'Survival and Success: the Kennedys of Dunure', in S. Boardman & A. Ross (eds) *The Exercise of Power in Medieval Scotland c. 1200–1500* (2003).

H. Potter *Bloodfeud: The Stewarts and Gordons at War* (2002)

C. Tabraham *Scotland's Castles* (2005)

J. Taylor *The Great Historic Families of Scotland* (1887–91)

O. Thomson *The Great Feud: The Campbells and the MacDonalds* (2000)

Published by Historic Scotland 2008

Printed from sustainable materials 2008

Crown copyright © 2008

ISBN 978 1 904966 97 5

Design Aukett Brockliss Guy Ltd

Principal photography Michael Brooks and David Henrie

Illustrations, pages 5, 6 and 8 © Mark D. Dennis

Illustrations, pages 23, 34 and 61 David Simon

Clansmen's crest badges © Art Pewter Silver Ltd of East Kilbride, reproduced by kind permission. Originally published in Micheil MacDonald *The Clans of Scotland* (1991).

Tartans kindly supplied by Geoffrey (Tailor), Kiltmakers and Weavers, 57 High Street, Edinburgh www.geoffreykilts.co.uk